REVOLUTIONARY WAR

PERIOD

COOKERY

A Unique Collection of Favorite Recipes from Notable People & Families in America's Glorious Past

Robert W. Pelton

Copyright © 2003 by Robert W. Pelton

ISBN 0-7414-1053-4

Published by:

PUBLISHING.COM

519 West Lancaster Avenue
Haverford, PA 19041-1413
Info@buybooksontheweb.com
www.buybooksontheweb.com
Toll-free (877) BUY BOOK
Local Phone (610) 520-2500
Fax (610) 519-0261

Printed in the United States of America

Printed on Recycled Paper

Published January, 2003

Part of the Pelton
Historical Cookbook Series

Includes the Following Titles:

Civil War Period Cookery
Historical Christmas Cookery
Historical Thanksgiving Cookery

COVERS SUCH CATEGORIES AS:

Heroes of the American Revolution
Foreign Friends of the Revolution
Signers of the Declaration of Independence
Signers of Our Constitution
Those Who Fought and Died for the Cause

INCLUDES THE FAVORITE RECIPES OF:

George Washington
Thomas Jefferson
Paul Revere
John Hancock
Betsy Ross
Benjamin Franklin
General Lafayette
Samuel Adams
Nathan Hale
Rebecca Motte
James Madison

Dedication

To Barnabus Horton of Leichestershire, England, who came to America on the ship, *Swallow,* some time between 1633 and 1638 with his wife Mary and two sons, Joseph and Benjamin. They landed at Hampton, Massachusetts, and were Puritans;

And to my Great-great grandmother Huldah Radike Horton, one of the finest and most famous horsewomen of her day. She rode with Lafayette in a parade in his honor in Newburg, New York, in 1824. The French General and friend of our young Republic was making his second and last visit.

CONTENTS

Introducing
Revolutionary War Period
Cookery

Revolutionary War Period Cookery is chock full of delightfully different and delicious cooking ideas favored by many famous, and some forgotten, yet historically important individuals and families of yesteryear. It contains the favorite dishes of numerous well known as well as lesser-known figures from the Revolutionary War period of our glorious history. Included are tasty breads and other baked goods, taste-tempting main dishes, soups and stews and loads of other wonderful recipes.

Here you will find the favorites of such historical luminaries as Alexander Hamilton who was born in the West Indies, but moved to the Colonies in 1772. He became one of the brightest stars in the fight for independence. One of George Washington's closest friends, this man dearly loved what was called Blood Bread with his dinners. A delightful Walnut Bread Pudding dish was eagerly eaten by General Lafayette in 1824 on his final visit to his beloved America. And those very special Sweet Potato Griddle Cakes were often prepared and served by the family of General Philip Schuyler.

Most early American recipes as originally written would be quite difficult, if not impossible, to use today with any degree of ease or accuracy. Such concoctions were most often written as one long and rather complicated, sometimes rambling paragraph. Or they might simply be a long list of ingredients in no particular sequence or order. And many of the ingredients called for would not be recognized by today's readers.

One of the most popular cakes, as well as the only cake made without bread dough in the Colonies, was that called **The Nun's Cake**. The recipe for this special cake was carefully cherished and handed down as a prized heirloom from prior generations. It was no doubt, often handwritten, and bequeathed from mother to daughter. Or, the ingredients may have been memorized, and passed along by word of mouth. The recipe for this highly regarded cake appears in almost all early cook books, with little or no variation of its ingredients or instructions as to how it was to be made in those days. Here it is:

"You must take four pounds of the finest flour, and three pounds of double-refined sugar beaten and sifted; mix them together and dry them by the fire till you prepare your other materials. Take four pounds of butter, beat it with your hand till it is soft like cream, then beat thirty-five eggs, leave out sixteen whites, strain off your eggs from the treads, and beat them and the butter together till all appears like butter. Put in four or five spoonfuls of rose or orange-flower water, and beat again; then take your flour and sugar, with six ounces of caraway-seeds, and strew them in by degrees, beating it up all the time for two hours together. You may put in as much tincture of cinnamon or amber-grease as you please; butter your hoop, and let it stand three hours in a moderate

oven. You must observe always, in beating of butter, to do it with a cool hand and beat it always one way in a deep earthen dish."

The ultimate in simplicity went into this description of an old favorite *"To Make Little Cakes For Tea."* But, alas, it certainly would not be so simple a task for today's lady of the house to make them successfully. Here are the complete instructions:

"Of butter, flower, sugar a quarter of a pound of each and as much yoke of egg as will mix into a stiff paste. Make them into round cakes the size of half a crown. Bake them in tins. Put some Caraway seeds in them."

The year 1796, a few years after the Revolutionary War, saw the publication of *American Cookery* by Amelia Simmons. In her book, this woman gave these fine examples for the homemaker of that day to use in making:

"A NICE INDIAN PUDDING:
"No. 1. 3 pints scalded milk, 7 spoons fine Indian meal, stir well together while hot, let stand till cooled; add 7 eggs, half pound raisins, 4 ounces butter, spice and sugar, bake one and half hour.
"No.2. 3 pints scalded milk to one pint meal salted; cool, add two eggs, 4 ounces butter, sugar or molasses and spice q.s. it will require two and half hours baking.
"No.3. Salt a pint meal, wet with one quart milk, sweeten and put into a strong cloth, brass or bell metal vessel or earthen pot, secure from wet and boil 12 hours."

Early American baking recipes might call for German or **Compressed Yeast, Patent Yeast, Brewers Yeast** or **Potato Yeast**. Some yeasts were made from hops or grape leaves. Such recipes are made much more practical for

3

today's homemakers to use by simply substituting the more modern versions of yeast – those small packets we can readily purchase in our supermarkets. Nevertheless, here's a unique old-time method for making yeast using grape leaves. My Great-great grandmother Huldah Radike Horton who once entertained and rode with the great French General Lafayette handed this down. This is exactly how she inscribed it in her own hand:

"YEAST FROM GRAPE LEAVES

"Grape leaves make a yeast in some respects superior to hops, as the bread made from it rises sooner, and has not the peculiar taste which many object to in that made from hops. Use eight or ten leaves for a quart of yeast; Boil them for ten minutes; Pour the hot liquor on the flour, the quantity of the latter being determined by whether the yeast in wanted thick or thin; Use the hop yeast to raise it with to begin with, and afterwards that made of grape leaves. Dried leaves will be as good as fresh. If a dark film appears upon the surface when rising, a little stirring will obviate it."

Measurements were given in ways that present day cooks aren't at all familiar: a teacupful, wineglassful, tincupful, kitchencupful, ½ a tumbler, 1 dram liquid, dessertspoonful , saltspoonful, butter the size of a walnut, butter the size of an egg, pound of eggs, pound of milk, gill, etc. Therefore, all the recipes herein have been carefully updated. When used by the homemaker of today, they will turn out just as they did for the woman of the house that prepared them so many long years ago. Here's a list of a few of the more unique measurements sometimes used by housewives and others during the Colonial period of our history. The original measurement is initially given followed by its modern day conversion:

Dessertspoonful	2 teaspoons
Saltspoonful	¼ teaspoon
1 gill	½ cup
1 fluid dram	1 teaspoon
Kitchencupful	1 cup
Teacupful	¾ cup
Coffecupful	1 cup
Tumbler	½ pint
Wineglassful	4 tablespoons
Dash pepper	⅛ teaspoon
Pound of milk	1 pint
Pound of eggs	12 medium eggs
	9 large eggs

As you probably know, James Monroe (1758-1831) bravely fought with the Continental Army during the first years of the War for Independence and was wounded at Trenton, New Jersey. He was sometime later the major man behind the writing of our magnificent *Constitution*. Monroe eventually got into national politics under the sponsorship of Thomas Jefferson and ultimately became the 5th President of the United States. Monroe was a Christian and in his inaugural address on March 4, 1817, he referred to God's overruling providence: ***"Except the Lord keep the city, the watchman waketh in vain."***

James Monroe enjoyed a special dish his wife, Elizabeth, called her *"Delicate Fritters."* And this is how they were made:

1 cup flour	**4 tbls sugar**
1-½ tsp baking powder	**1 egg yolk, beaten**
2 tbls cornstarch	**⅓ cup milk**
¼ tsp salt	**1 tbls olive oil**

1 egg white, beaten

Sift together the dry ingredients in a wooden mixing bowl. Repeat the sifting three times. Alternately stir in the beaten egg yolk and milk. Add the olive oil and beat until smooth. Fold in the stiffly beaten egg whites. Set aside while you heat a frying pan of cooking oil. Lastly, drop the fritter mixture by large spoonfuls into the hot oil. Fry until golden brown. Turn them once. When done, lay fritters on absorbent paper to drain. Dust with powdered sugar. Serve while hot.

The above was Mrs. Monroe's basic recipe for plain fritters. For variety she would add fruit pieces to the batter. Or she might toss in chopped vegetable pieces, clams or oysters. In so doing, she would add more milk to her batter *"ever so slightly."* This particular recipe makes around 10 good size fritters.

Every unique recipe found in this book was popular during, or at least the favorite concoction of, some notable personality during the Revolutionary War Period. Many were coveted within a famous family of that historical era and handed down from one generation to the next. All are historical gems, for each was the invention of, or the culinary specialty of, some family or individual of days long gone by. Here they are presented, for the first time, for America's families of today to have the fun, and experience the thrill of, cooking and baking and serving. And lastly, to thankfully pass a blessing over before eating these special treats – be it for part of a unique breakfast, lunch or dinner.

1

Griddle Cakes and Flapjacks Enjoyed by Heroes of the Past

Bread Pancake Receipt of Mrs. Otis

2-½ cups breadcrumbs, dry	1 tbls shortening, melted
1 egg yolk	2 cups flour
¾ cup milk	2 tsp salt
¾ cup water	3 tsp baking powder
1 egg white, stiffly beaten	

Soak the dry breadcrumbs in water until soft. Squeeze as dry as possible. Then crumble and measure into a large wooden mixing bowl. Beat together thoroughly the egg yolk, milk, water, bread crumbs and melted shortening. In a separate bowl sift together the flour, salt and baking powder. Add this to the first mixture and blend well. Lastly fold in the stiffly beaten egg white. Drop by tablespoonfuls onto a hot griddle. Cook until nicely browned on both sides. Makes 12 servings.

** ** ** ** **

James Otis (1725-83) was one of many forgotten heroic Christian patriots of the American Revolution. This brave man was a great orator in his day, one that stood for freedom when it counted the most. He was known to be an eloquent lawyer who was called a "*flame of fire*" by his peers. Otis was a cousin of the scholarly John Adams. He fearlessly fought early on with a passion against unfair British taxation on shipments sent abroad by Massachusetts's merchants.

Sweet Milk Griddle Cakes as Made by Mrs. Knox

1-½ cups flour   1 egg, beaten
1 tbls sugar   1 cup milk
2 tbls shortening, melted

Sift the flour with the sugar in a wooden mixing bowl and set aside. Combine the beaten egg, milk and melted shortening in another bowl and blend well. Add the dry ingredients to these and beat thoroughly until smooth. Use ladle and pour into small, greased cast iron skillet. Lightly brown on one side and then flip over to lightly brown on the other. Then follow the tips as given below.

Griddle Cake Tips as Given by Mrs. Knox

Mrs. Knox always used a cast iron skillet for making her families griddlecakes or pancakes for breakfast. Here's how she explains her technique: *"Heat the skillet and put in a teaspoon of lard or butter. Let it melt and run over the bottom of the skillet. Then pour in a ladleful of batter. It should be enough to cover the bottom of the skillet.with a thin sheet. Cook and turn over with a tin spatula, very carefully, to avoid tearing the griddlecake.*

"When griddle cake is done, have a hot dish ready. Turn out griddlecake on dish. Sprinkle with powdered sugar. Roll griddlecake up dexterously like a sheet of paper. Keep griddlecakes hot by setting the dish in the oven until enough are cooked. Send one-half dozen to the table at once."

** ** ** ** **

Henry Knox (1750-1806) was a leading General during the American War for Independence. This devout Christian leader was one of George Washington's most trusted friends and advisors. Born and raised in Boston of Scot-Irish heritage, Knox was active early on in the Revolutionary movement with his involvement with the Boston militia. He fought heroically at Bunker Hill and in almost every major battle during the Revolutionary War. Knox was promoted to the rank of Major General after the British defeat at Yorktown. Washington appointed his long time friend to be the first Secretary of War under the newly written American *Constitution.*

Rice Pancakes – A Samuel Adams Favorite

1 cup rice, boiled until tender	2 tbls sugar
2 cups milk	1-½ tbls baking powder
1 egg, well beaten	1 cup flour
2 tsp salt	3 tbls butter, melted

Put the boiled rice into a large wooden mixing bowl. Blend in the milk, frothy beaten egg, salt and sugar. In a separate bowl sift together the baking powder and flour. Stir this into the first mixture. Lastly blend in the melted butter. Beat thoroughly to a creamy batter. Drop batter into hot well-greased cast iron skillet by large spoonfuls. Lightly brown on both sides. Serve while steaming hot with butter and syrup or sugar.

** ** ** ** **

Samuel Adams (1722-1803) is best known in history as the *"Father of the American Revolution."* This great man was the driving force behind the Boston Tea Party. He and his cousin, John Adams, were both heroic signers of the *Declaration of Independence.* Both had been well-known patriots and leaders in the Colonies for more than 20 years. When the *Declaration of Independence* was signed in 1776, Adams declared: *"We have this day restored the Sovereign to whom all men ought to be obedient. He reigns in heaven and from the rising to the setting of the sun, let His kingdom come."*

12

Philip John Schuyler's Favorite Sweet Potato Griddle Cakes

1 cup sweet potatoes, boiled and mashed	2 tsp salt
	2 tbls sugar
2 cups milk	1-½ tbls baking powder
3 eggs, well beaten	1-½ cups flour
3 tbls butter, melted	

Put the mashed sweet potatoes into a large wooden mixing bowl. Blend in the milk, frothy beaten eggs, salt and sugar. Sift together the baking powder and flour in a separate bowl. Stir this into the first mixture. Lastly add the melted butter and blend everything thoroughly. Beat to a creamy batter. Use a ladle and drop batter into a hot well-greased cast iron skillet. Lightly brown on both sides. Serve hot with butter and maple syrup or brown sugar.

** ** ** ** **

Philip John Schuyler (1733-1804) fought in the French and Indian War as a Captain in the British Army in 1756. He later served under George Washington as a General in the Continental Army. Said to be better suited for a desk job than a battlefield command, Major General Schuyler apparently had much difficulty making decisions under pressure. He was often reported to abdicate his responsibilities, but not his command, to his subordinates. He would retire to his tent with "a bilious fever and violent rheumatic pains" when important decisions had to me made. Nevertheless, Schuyler, a Christian, was highly thought of by his peers and was selected to be a member of the Continental Assembly in 1768. And he was also chosen to hold the important position as a delegate to the Continental Congress in 1775.

Ultra Rich Pancakes – A Reed Family Specialty

4 cups flour	3 eggs, well beaten
4 tsp baking powder	½ cup heavy cream
1 tsp salt	1-½ cups water

Sift together the flour, baking powder and salt in a large wooden mixing bowl. In a separate bowl blend together the beaten eggs, heavy cream and water. Stir this in with the first mixture. Beat thoroughly to a creamy batter. This batter should be quite thick. Use a ladle and drop batter into a hot well-greased cast iron skillet. Lightly brown on both sides. Serve while hot with butter and maple syrup or other syrup of choice.

** ** ** ** **

Joseph Reed (? – 1775) of Philadelphia was George Washington's Adjutant General and one of his trusted advisors during the American War for Independence. This devout Christian was the one person most responsible for exposing the treason of General Benedict Arnold. And Reed was also the man who forced the bringing of Arnold to trial for his traitorous activities.

Stale Bread Hot Cakes as Prepared by the Revere Family

1-½ cups bread crumbs, stale   2 eggs, well beaten
1-½ cups milk, scalded   ½ cup flour
2 tbls butter, melted   ½ tsp salt
             1-½ tbls baking powder

Put the stale breadcrumbs in large wooden mixing bowl. Add hot milk and melted butter and mix lightly. Allow to soak until crumbs are soft. Then stir in the frothy beaten eggs. Sift together the flour, salt and baking powder in a separate bowl. Blend this into the first mixture. Beat thoroughly to a creamy batter. Using a ladle, drop batter into a hot well-greased cast iron skillet. Cook until lightly browned. Turn once and lightly brown other side. Serve while steaming hot with butter and syrup or sprinkled with sugar.

** ** ** ** **

Paul Revere (1735-1818) is certainly a man never to be forgotten in American history. A silversmith by trade, and Boston's best, this Christian, church-going patriot rode through Lexington to warn those who were protecting Samuel Adams and John Hancock of impending danger. The British forces were on the way! Then, having finished his all-important task at hand, this heroic patriot bravely rode on through the countryside warning his fellow Americans of the approaching Redcoats.

Buttermilk Pancakes
as Made by the Motte Family

2 eggs, well-beaten	1 tsp salt
2 cups buttermilk	1 tsp sugar
2 cups flour	1 tbls lard, melted
¼ cup yellow corn meal	1 tbls butter, melted
1 tsp baking powder	1 tsp baking soda

Put the frothy beaten eggs and the buttermilk in a large wooden mixing bowl and blend together thoroughly. Sift in the flour, corn meal, baking powder, salt and sugar. Mix everything well. Lastly stir in the melted lard, melted butter and baking soda dissolved in warm water. Blend thoroughly to a creamy batter. Using a ladle or large spoon, drop batter into a hot well-greased cast iron skillet. Lightly brown on one side, flip over and lightly brown on the other side. Serve while piping hot with butter and syrup or sprinkle with sugar.

** ** ** ** **

Rebecca, a church-going Christian girl had sailed from England to marry Jacob Motte, a wealthy South Carolina planter. The adventuresome young lady was a widow by the time the Revolutionary War began. She was forced to abandon her mansion when it was occupied by the British and used as their headquarters. They renamed it Fort Motte. In retaliation, this feisty patriot purchased a bow from some Indians. She then proceeded to hire an expert marksman to shoot fiery arrows at her mansion and burn it to the ground.

2

Old-Time Soups and Chowders

Cream of Celery Soup
A Baldwin Family Favorite

1 cup celery, diced	3 tbls flour
1 cup water, boiling	2-½ cups milk, scalded
1 tbls onion, minced	Salt to suit taste
3 tbls butter, melted	Pepper to suit taste

Combine celery and water in a small soup kettle. Cover and let simmer until celery is tender. Meanwhile, put the minced onion and melted butter in another small pot and cook until lightly browned. Add the flour and mix until smooth. Then slowly add the milk, stirring constantly. Cook mixture over a pot of hot water until smooth and thick. Lastly stir in the celery and water in which it was cooked. Add salt and pepper to taste. Heat thoroughly and serve while hot. Makes six servings.

** ** ** ** **

Abraham Baldwin (1754-1807) is best remembered as a signer of the United States *Constitution*. A graduate of Yale and a brilliant scholar, Baldwin was in 1781 offered the professorship in divinity there. This man was a patriot who served as chaplain in the Continental Army during the Revolutionary War. Baldwin went on to found the University of Georgia and was its first president. A devout Christian, he believed it to be in the country's best interest *"to support the principles of religion and morality."*

Pigeon Soup as Enjoyed by Thomas Jefferson

2 pigeons, cut up   ½ pint cream
2 quarts water, boiling   ½ cup bread crumbs
4 sprigs parsley   Salt to suit taste
½ cup spinach, chopped fine   Mace to suit taste

Put pigeon pieces in cooking pot with boiling water and allow to simmer for 3 hours. Strain and set pigeon pieces aside to drain and cool. Now add parsley and spinach to the stock in the pot. Blend cream and bread crumbs in a bowl. Add this to pot with other ingredients and stir well. Set aside while you cut pigeon meat into small pieces. Season lightly to taste with salt and mace. Put back into soup mixture and let simmer for 15 minutes. Serve while steaming hot.

** ** ** ** **

Thomas Jefferson (1743-1826) was the first United States Secretary of State and Second Vice President. He was the 3rd President who served his country in this position from 1801 to 1809. Jefferson was a brilliant inventor and was known to have limitless intellectual curiosity. Thomas Jefferson died on July 4th, the 50th anniversary of the signing of the *Declaration of Independence*, the magnificent

21

document he had authored. Was this great man a Christian. Many historians say no! But let Jefferson answer this question himself: " *I am a real Christian; that is to say, a disciple of the doctrines of Jesus. I am a Christian in the only sense in which He wished any one to be; sincerely attached to His doctrines in preference to all others.* "

The Pearson Family's Carrot Soup Recipe

2 tbls butter	3-½ cups carrots, sliced
1 large onion, sliced	1 cup celery, chopped fine
1 tbls flour	2 tsp salt
4 cups beef or veal broth	¼ tsp pepper

Melt the butter in a large cast iron soup kettle. Then lay in the sliced onion pieces and cook until they are nicely browned. Stir in the flour and add the meat broth. Mix everything thoroughly. Now add carrots, celery, salt and pepper. Stir and cover pot. Let simmer on stove for 2-1/2 hours. Strain through a sieve and serve immediately while steaming hot.

** ** ** ** **

Theodore Pearson was an honest Christian businessman who was long ago forgotten in American history. But he was a man who made an important contribution nonetheless. If not for Mr. Pearson, we may not have crackers in our supermarkets today. This man opened America's first cracker factory in Newburyport, Massachusetts, way back in 1792.

A Gerry Family Favorite – Salmon Chowder

2 tbls bacon, diced	1 tbls butter
1 small onion, chopped	2 bouillon cubes
1 cup potatoes, diced	Salt to suit taste
1 cup tomatoes, cooked	Pepper to suit taste
2 cups salmon, shredded	2 cups water

Brown the bacon in a hot cast iron skillet. Add onion and simmer until lightly browned. Next stir in diced potatoes, tomatoes, water, butter, and bouillon cubes. Cover skillet and allow mixture to simmer until potatoes are tender. Season to taste with salt and pepper. Lastly, stir in shredded salmon and blend everything thoroughly. Serve at once while hot. Makes enough to feed 6 people.

** ** ** ** **

Elbridge Gerry (1744-1814) of Massachusetts is an important but often forgotten man in American history. He was the Vice President of the United States under President James Madison from 1813 to 1814. This devout Christian was a delegate at the Constitutional Convention in Philadelphia where he is known to have spoken 119 times. Gerry was one of the heroic 56 signers of the *Declaration of Independence*. Of the 42 delegates present at the end of the

Constitutional Convention on September 17, 1787, all but three signed the *Constitution*. The three who refused were Mason, Randolph and Gerry. They were all fearful of a powerful centralized government.

Navy Bean Soup – One of Nathan Hale's Boyhood Favorites

1-½ cups navy beans	1 carrot, diced
4 cups water, cold	2-½ cups milk
¼ pound salt pork	2 tsp salt
1 small onion, diced	¼ tsp pepper
½ cup celery, diced	¼ tsp paprika

Wash beans carefully and put in cast iron soup kettle. Cover with cold water. Add the salt pork and bring to boil. Let simmer for about 2 hours. Then add onion, celery and carrot before beans are tender. Cook for about another hour. When beans are soft, take out the salt pork and pour mixture from kettle through a sieve. Add salt, pepper and paprika to the pulp. Cut salt pork into very small cubes and put back into soup. Stir well and reheat mixture. Serve while steaming hot. Makes enough to serve 6 people.

** ** ** ** **

Nathan Hale (1755-76), a young Christian patriot, was a true American hero during the Revolutionary War. He had bravely volunteered for a dangerous mission behind enemy lines. Fully aware of the consequences if he were to be captured, the 21 year old army captain went ahead anyway out of love for his country. Hale was captured by the British and soon after executed as a spy on September 22, 1776. In a journal written by British Lieutenant MacKenzie, it was reported that this young man *"behaved with great composure saying he thought it the duty of every good officer to obey any orders given him by his Commander-in-Chief."* Nathan Hale went bravely to his death by hanging in an apple orchard. One of the last things he asked for was a *Bible*. The British denied his request. His last words were: *"I regret that I have but one life to give for my country."*

Clam Soup as Served to John Hancock

2 dozen clams, chopped   Salt to suit taste
1 quart milk   Pepper to suit taste
1 small onion, chopped   Butter to suit
6 stalks celery, chopped   Whipped cream to suit
Chopped parsley to suit taste

Put chopped clam pieces in large soup kettle with their own liquor or juice and bring to a quick boil. In a separate pot, scald the milk with the onion and celery in it. Let this mixture simmer for 5 minutes and then strain off the milk. Add the milk to the clams in the kettle just before serving. Do this gradually so the milk will not curdle. Season to taste with salt and pepper. Put small piece of butter in each cup before serving. Garnish with whipped cream and finely chopped parsley. Makes enough for 8 servings.

** ** ** ** **

John Hancock (1737-93) was without doubt one of the greatest of our Christian Founding Fathers. He was the first man to sign the *Declaration of Independence*. Hancock boldly exclaimed as he penned his name on the document: ***"There! His Majesty can now read my name without spectacles, and can now double his reward of 500 pounds for my head. That is my defiance!"*** He gained a great deal of lasting fame for placing the largest signature on the document. This brave man served as President of the Second Continental Congress, and he later became the first elected Governor of Massachusetts. Hancock's final great service to his nation was to have the honor of presiding over the Massachusetts Convention when it ratified the *United States Constitution*. While Governor of Massachusetts, on November 8, 1783, Hancock issued a Thanksgiving proclamation to celebrate the victorious end of the War for American Independence. It said in part: ***"... the citizens of these United States have every Reason for Praise and Gratitude to the God of their Salvation."***

Mrs. Hart's Special Squash Soup

3 tbls butter, melted	4 tbls flour
1-½ cups squash, cooked	1-½ tsp salt
3 cups heavy cream	¼ tsp pepper
2 tsp parsley, chopped fine	

Blend melted butter and flour in a soup kettle. Add heavy cream (or milk) and cook, stirring constantly, until slightly thickened. Then thoroughly mash the cooked squash. Put squash, salt, pepper and chopped parsley into the kettle with the other ingredients and mix well. Let it all simmer for about 10 minutes. Serve while piping hot. Makes enough delicious soup to feed 5 people.

** ** ** ** **

John Hart (1711-79) was another Christian patriot who bravely signed the *Declaration of Independence*. In retaliation, the vengeful British drove this heroic man from his dying wife's bedside. Their 13 children fled for their lives, never to be seen again. Hart was forced to live in woods and caves to hide from the British for more than a year. He finally was able to return home only to find that everyone in his family had vanished. The exhausted man died of a broken heart a few weeks later.

3

Tasty Vegetable Dishes the Old-Fashioned Way

Mashed Turnips and Potato Dish – A Franklin Favorite

2 large potatoes, quartered   2 tbls flour
2 large turnips, quartered   1-½ tsp salt
4 tbls butter   ¼ tsp pepper
              ¼ cup water, cold

Put quartered potatoes and turnips in large pot and cover with water. Add salt and bring to a boil. Let cook until tender. Drain and mash to a pulp. Melt butter in another pot. Blend in flour, salt and pepper. Add cold water slowly while constantly stirring. Lastly blend in the mashed potato and turnip mixture from the first pot. Beat thoroughly until light and fluffy. Serve immediately. Makes enough to feed 6 people.

** ** ** ** **

Benjamin Franklin (1706-90) has the distinction of being the oldest signer of the *Declaration of Independence* at 70 while Edward Rutledge at 26 was the youngest. The 56 men who signed this marvelous document were considered to be the elite of the Colonies. Franklin was one of America's most influential statesmen in his day. He was also a signer of the *Constitution*. This great patriot taught himself five languages and was responsible for bringing France into the Revolutionary War on the side of the Colonies. Franklin once wrote: *"Here is my creed. I believe in God, the Creator of the Universe. That He governs it by His Providence. That He ought to be worshipped."*

The Wayne Family Stuffed Cabbage

1 medium head cabbage	1 egg, well beaten
1 cup ham, ground	1 tbls bacon grease
1 cup bread crumbs	Salt to suit taste
2 tbls onion, chopped	Pepper to suit taste
1 tbls parsley, chopped	3 tbls butter, melted
1 cup water, hot	

Put head of cabbage in cooking kettle and cover with cold salt water. Set aside and let soak for 1 hour. Then bring to boil and cook until almost tender. Take from pot and drain. Remove center from cabbage head, leaving 2 layers of leaves. Shred the portion of the cabbage that was removed. Now put the ground ham, breadcrumbs, chopped onions, parsley, beaten egg and bacon grease in a large wooden mixing bowl. Blend together thoroughly. Season with salt and pepper to taste. Pack this mixture lightly into cabbage shell. Tie the leaves tightly to hold stuffing in place. Put in small roaster. Baste with melted butter that has been combined with the hot water. Bake at 350 degrees for about 35 minutes. Makes 6 servings.

** ** ** ** **

General Anthony Wayne (1745-96), a man with strong Christian convictions, was a famous commander during the Revolutionary War. He became known as "Mad Anthony" due to his aggressive and dashing bravery in battle. General Wayne was instrumental in stopping the Indian uprisings in the West in 1794 and 1795. In June of 1779, the British captured a small but most important fort at Stony Point, New York, a short distance from the key American fortifications at West Point. Their intent was to use this in an effort to split the American colonies with a thrust up the Hudson Valley. But General Wayne had other ideas. He fearlessly attacked and captured the British held fort with only 1,350 men using unloaded guns and only bayonets. This man was the hero of the storming and retaking of Stony Point for the Americans on July 15, 1779.

The Putnam Family's Baked Sweet Potatoes

3 large sweet potatoes ½ cup butter, melted
2 eggs ¾ cup molasses
½ cup milk ⅛ tsp nutmeg
⅛ tsp cinnamon

Peel raw sweet potatoes and grate or chop fine. Put in large wooden mixing bowl. Add eggs, milk, melted butter, molasses, nutmeg and cinnamon. Blend everything thoroughly. Spoon into buttered baking dish. Bake at 375 degrees until center is firm and top is glazed over.

** ** ** ** **

General Israel Putnam (1718-90) was a great American *Bible* believing Christian patriot who was involved in many important battles during the War for Independence. This outstanding military leader was in charge of defending Philadelphia. Putnam was also a prominent figure at the famed Battle of Bunker Hill on June 17, 1775, where he told the militiamen: *"You are all marksmen. Don't fire until you see the whites of their eyes."* His orders were followed with devastating results. Although the battle ended in a victory for the British, the. redcoats lost 1,150 men while the colonists lost only 411 including their leader, Boston physician General Joseph Warren.

Colonial Greens Custard – A Favorite of "Lighthorse" Harry Lee

2 cups cooked greens	2 eggs, well beaten
1-½ tsp salt	1 tsp onion, chopped fine
¼ tsp pepper	1-½ cups soft breadcrumbs

1-½ cups milk

Drain cooked greens and chop medium fine. Put in a wooden mixing bowl and add salt, pepper, beaten eggs, chopped onion, breadcrumbs and milk. Blend everything thoroughly. Spoon mixture into buttered custard cups or 6 x 10-inch baking pan. Set custard cups or baking pan in larger pan containing 1 inch of water. Bake for 45 minutes in pre-heated 375 degree oven. Unmold from cups or cut into squares in baking pan. Serve while hot with creamed hard-boiled eggs. Makes enough to feed 6 people.

** ** ** ** **

"Lighthorse" Harry Lee (1756-1818) was an outstanding General during the Revolutionary War. Known to be a devout Christian, Lee was a close personal friend of George Washington. After Washington died about 10:00 p.m. on December 14, 1779, this great leader was given the honor of delivering the eulogy at the memorial ceremony in the nation's capitol. It was the day after Christmas when Lee spoke those never to be forgotten words: *"First in war, first in peace and first in the hearts of his countrymen, he was second to none."* He later went on to become the Governor of Virginia from 1792 to 1795.

Buttered Greens – A Ross Family Favorite

Allow ½ pound of green leaves for each person. Leaves of dandelion, mustard, kale, turnip, chard, spinach, chicory, etc., can be used. Look them over carefully. Remove all discolored and bruised leaves and throw away. Cut off roots and any tough stems. Also throw away. Select only fresh, tender and crisp leaves with bright coloring. Carefully wash leaves in seven waters. The first two should be warm to remove sand and dirt. Remove from the last water, sprinkle with salt and place in large kettle without water other than what clings to the leaves from washing. Cover kettle. Cook over low heat and let leaves steam until tender – about 15 to 20 minutes, depending on type of greens. Be careful not to overcook.

Turn greens in kettle occasionally while steaming. Drain a little if necessary. A small piece of salt pork or bacon (chopped fine) may be cooked with the greens if desired. Season to taste with bacon drippings or butter, vinegar or lemon juice. Sprinkle with salt and pepper as desired.

** ** ** ** **

Betsy Ross (1752-1836) was one of 17 children brought up in a staunch Quaker family. Her father, Samuel Grissom, helped build Independence Hall. She married John Ross, a non-Quaker, and was expelled from her sect. Betsy was a twice widowed seamstress of 25 who lived in Philadelphia when asked to make our first flag. According to her grandson, this very attractive young lady produced the first Stars and Stripes in 1776 when: *"A band of Continental leaders called upon my grandmother and asked her to undertake a special task. They probably selected her because George Washington was one of her patrons; she sewed many shirt ruffles for him about the time he was made Commander-in-Chief."*

Creamed Onions as Prepared by Mrs. Bedford

4 cups onions, sliced thin	Pinch of pepper
2 tbls butter	¼ cup cream
2 tbls flour	¼ cup cheese, grated
½ tsp salt	¼ garlic clove, grated

¼ cup liquid drained off onions

Put sliced onions and ½ cup water in small pot and cook until tender. Meanwhile, melt butter in another pot. Stir in flour, salt and pepper. Mix until smooth. Gradually add cream and let cook slowly until mixture thickens. Now add grated cheese, grated garlic and liquid from onions. Continue stirring until cheese melts. Pour this sauce over onions and serve immediately.

** ** ** ** **

Gunning Bedford (1747-1812) is a man often forgotten with the passage of time, but he was an instrumental force in American history. This great patriot was the Delaware delegate to the Constitutional Convention and a signer of the *Constitution*. While attending Princeton, he and James Madison were close friends and roommates. And he was one of many prominent Americans who studied under John Witherspoon, a man who was widely known to be the country's leading legal scholar and theologian of the period. Bedford, a devout Christian, believed that the *Bible* was ***"given by divine inspiration,"*** and he openly professed his faith ***"in God the Father, and in Jesus Christ, His only Son."***

38

The Allen Family Squash Cookery Secrets

Baked Acorn Squash or *Baked Winter Squash* is relatively easy to prepare according to these simple Allen family instructions. Cut squash into pieces desirable for serving. Remove seeds and stringy portion. Discard these. Place squash pieces in dripping pan. Sprinkle with salt and pepper. Spread 1 teaspoon molasses over each piece of squash. Then add ½ teaspoon butter. Bake 50 minutes or until soft in a 350 degree oven Keep pan covered the first 30 minutes of baking. Then bake 20 minutes more while uncovered. Serve hot in the shell.

Steamed Winter Squash is delightful. Scrub squash and cut in pieces. Remove seeds and stringy portion. Peel if possible. If not, steam over boiling water for 30 to 40 minutes, or until squash is tender. Then remove peel if it is still on squash. Put squash through a sieve. Beat thoroughly. Season to taste with salt, pepper and butter. Beat again. Serve while hot.

** ** ** ** **

Ethan Allen (1737-89) and his five companies of Green Mountain Boys heroically defeated the British at Fort Ticonderoga in 1775. Not a man to mince words, Allen called for the surrender of the Fort *"in the name of the*

Great Jehovah and the Continental Congress." This flamboyant, sword waving, hotheaded Vermont farmer, became everybody's hero throughout the Colonies. The name Ethan Allen was known in every household. This 6'-6'' brawler had a reputation for strangling wildcats with his bare hands. A patriot and a Christian of the first order, Allen once said: *"Ever since I arrived to a state of manhood, I have felt a sincere passion for liberty."*

4

Stews, Pot Pies and Casseroles from Another Era

Steak and Kidney Pudding Pie – A Sherman Family Specialty

First Prepare the Crust

1-½ cups flour	1 tsp baking powder
⅔ tsp salt	½ cup beef suet, chopped fine
	Ice cold water to suit

Sift together the flour, salt and baking powder in a wooden mixing bowl. Stir in the finely chopped suet. Moisten with enough ice water to make a stiff dough. Cut off a piece of the dough and set aside to later make a top crust. Roll the remainder out thin on a well-floured board. Use this to line a well-greased baking pan. Set aside and prepare the meat filling as follows:

1-½ pounds beef, lean	1 cup flour
2 sheep's kidneys	2-½ tbls salt
or	2-½ tbls pepper
½ beef kidney	Cold water to suit

Slice beef into thin strips. Blend together the flour, salt and pepper in a wooden mixing bowl. Coat each strip by rolling it around in this mixture. Place a small piece of kidney on each beef strip and roll it up tightly. Pack these in the pastry lined baking pan. When fully packed, fill ⅔ full of water. Wet the edges of the crust. Cover with the reserved dough rolled out to fit top of baking pan. Tie a floured cloth over the top. Place baking pan in larger pan containing enough boiling water to come ⅔ of the way up the sides of first pan. Boil for at least 3 hours. Add more water to that in pan as it boils away. When done, turn out the potpie. Cut hole in top of crust and pour a cup of water into it to make additional gravy. Serve piping hot.

** ** ** ** **

Roger Sherman (1721-93) was a notable Christian patriot leader during the Colonial period of our glorious history. He is the *only* one of the Founding Fathers to sign all four of the major founding documents. These were: 1774 – *The Articles of Association*; 1776 – *The Declaration of Independence*; 1777 – *The Articles of Confederation*; 1787 – *The United States Constitution*. Sherman was a leading member of the Continental Congress and made an astounding 138 speeches at the Constitutional Convention. He was also the man who seconded the motion made by Benjamin Franklin that Congress be opened each day with prayer.

General Pulaski's Favorite Bigos
(Hunter's Stew)

2-½ pounds sauerkraut	3 cups polish sausage,
1 cup fresh mushrooms,	sliced thin
sliced	3 cups cooked meat,
½ cup bacon, diced	cut in ½ inch chunks
4 sprigs parsley,	1 cup meat gravy
chopped	½ tsp salt
1 large onion,	½ tsp pepper
chopped	2 tbls sugar
2 tsp flour	¾ cup hot water

1 cup wine (red or white)

Wash sauerkraut and lay it in large cooking pot. Stir in mushrooms. Cover pot and allow sauerkraut to simmer 30 minutes. Meanwhile, put the bacon, parsley and onion in a cast iron skillet and fry while constantly stirring mixture until onion turns a light golden brown. Add flour. Mix well and smooth out with a little of the sauerkraut juice from the cooking pot. Then pour this mixture into the sauerkraut and blend thoroughly. Mix together the sausage slices and cooked meat cubes. Carefully fold these into the sauerkraut in the cooking pot. Season meat gravy with salt, pepper and sugar. Add this to the other ingredients in the cooking pot. Now add the hot water, cover pot, and allow everything to simmer on the stove for 45 minutes. Lastly, stir in the wine and bring stew to a boil. Immediately remove pot from stove and set aside to cool. Makes enough to fill 8 people. **NOTE:** *This stew should not be eaten until the day after it is cooked. It is then to be warmed up and served with boiled potatoes.*

** ** ** ** **

General Casimir Pulaski (1748-79) arrived in the Colonies in July of 1777, ready to fight and to die for freedom and liberty. This great Christian patriot so believed in the American cause that he donated more than $50,000 of his own money to form the famed "Pulaski Legion." In October of 1779, British troops in Savannah, Georgia, came under siege by American forces under the command of General Benjamin Lincoln. On October 9th, the Continental Army's Polish Military Advisor, Count Kazimierz Pulaski, led his cavalry in a charge at the British lines. He was mortally wounded and died on October 11th. Yes, this man unselfishly and heroically gave his life for the great American cause of liberty and freedom at the age of only 31.

Venison Stew – As Enjoyed by the Pinckney Family

First Make the Marinade:

1 medium onion, sliced thin	3 cups red wine
¾ cup cider vinegar	2 tsp salt
1 bay leaf	½ tsp pepper
3 garlic cloves, minced	3 tbls warm honey
1 carrot, chopped	3 whole cloves

Put all of the above ingredients in a large wooden mixing bowl and blend thoroughly. Set aside while preparing the stew as follows:

3 pounds venison	1 cup tomatoes, mashed
4 tbls butter	1 large onion, sliced thin
1-½ tsp salt	1 green bell pepper, sliced
¼ tsp pepper	1 cup water
Flour to suit	

Trim all excess fat from the venison. Cut meat into one-inch cubes. Place in a large cooking pot. Pour marinade over the meat. Cover pot and set aside on ice for 24 hours or more. Stir mixture of venison and marinade three of four times while on ice. Then take venison from pot and let drain on paper. Meanwhile, melt butter in a large cast iron skillet. Put drained venison pieces in skillet and slowly brown on all sides. When all pieces are nicely browned, stir in strained marinade from mixing bowl. Add salt and pepper. Cover skillet and let mixture simmer gently for 1-1/2 hours. Then add tomatoes, onion, green bell pepper and ½ cup water to skillet. Let simmer 1 more hour. Thicken sauce with flour that has been blended to a paste with remaining ½ cup of water. Let mixture simmer for another 10 minutes and then serve immediately. Makes enough to feed 6 people.

** ** ** ** **

Thomas Pinckney (1750-1828) fought with the Continental Army under General George Washington during the War for American Independence. This great Christian leader was wounded at the Battle of Camden and taken prisoner by the British. Pinckney served as Governor of South Carolina after the Revolutionary War. He was the man who presided over the convention that ratified the Constitution. Educated in England as a young man, he later was appointed as minister to Great Britain and served in this important position from 1792 to 1796.

Tongue Casserole as Enjoyed by General Sullivan

1 beef tongue	1 cup celery, diced
2 tbls flour	1 cup turnips, diced
2 tbls bacon grease	1 cup carrots, diced
1 tsp salt	1 cup peas, cooked
¼ tsp pepper	1 cup potatoes, diced
1 tsp onions, minced	

Wash tongue and put into kettle of water. Bring to boil and cook until tender. Take from pot and remove skin. Lay tongue in casserole pan or dish. In wooden mixing bowl, combine flour, baking grease and 2 cups of the broth from kettle in which tongue was cooked. Add salt and pepper. Blend everything thoroughly. Set this aside while arranging celery, turnips, carrots, peas, potatoes and onions around tongue in casserole pan. Pour over this mixture the sauce previously made with the broth. Bake at 400 degrees until vegetables are tender.

** ** ** ** **

General John Sullivan (1740-95), born in Berwick, Maine, is a forgotten American hero. This man proudly served with General George Washington's Continental Army during the American War for Independence. He was a steadfast patriot and a Christian. True to the cause of freedom, Sullivan was a member of the First Continental Congress. When rebellion reared its ugly head in 1787 New Hampshire, Sullivan, then Governor, quickly took decisive action to stop it before it got out of hand.

Mrs. Jay's Thanksgiving Leftover Turkey Pot Pie

5-½ cups turkey broth	1 cup peas
4 carrots, scraped	¾ cup butter
1 onion, diced	1 cup flour
1 garlic clove, minced	Salt to suit taste
½ pound mushrooms, sliced	Pepper to suit taste
6 cups cooked turkey, bite size pieces	

Put turkey broth in large cooking pot. Cut carrots in 1 inch pieces and add to broth with onion. Bring to boil and then let simmer until almost tender. Now add minced garlic, mushrooms and peas. Let simmer 5 to 10 minutes longer. Take vegetables out of pot and set aside. Also set aside 4 cups of the broth.

Now put butter in cooking pot with remaining turkey broth and slowly add flour while whisking it to avoid lumping. Let simmer while constantly stirring for 3 minutes. Gradually whisk in the other 4 cups broth previously set aside. Continue simmering until mixture bubbles and thickens. Stir in salt and pepper to suit taste.

Pour ¼ inch deep layer of this gravy into bottom of baking pan. Put equal amount of gravy in wooden mixing bowl and set aside to use later. Blend turkey pieces and vegetables in kettle with remaining gravy. Pour this into baking pan. Cover with gravy previously set aside in mixing bowl. Put on ice to cool. Now make a crust as follows:

1 cup flour	3 tbls ice water
½ tsp salt	1 egg yolk
6 tbls butter	1 tbls cream

Blend flour and salt in wooden mixing bowl. Cut butter in with a fork until flour mixture is coarse and crumbly.

49

Slowly add ice water and blend with fork until dough is moist enough to hold together nicely. Turn out on lightly floured board and knead until dough is smooth. Wrap in oiled paper and put on ice to chill for 1 hour.

When ready, roll dough out again on floured board to ¼ inch thick. Cut to fit baking pan. Allow enough to hang over edges of pan at least 1 inch. Lay dough over filling in baking pan. Tuck edges of crust under. Press dough against sides of baking pan to seal well. Cut hole in middle of dough about 1 inch in diameter for steam outlet.

Lastly, blend egg yolk and cream in small bowl. Coat dough on top of pot pie with this mixture by brushing it on. Bake at 350 degrees for 40 minutes or until crust browns nicely. Serves 6 to 8 people.

** ** ** ** **

John Jay (1745-1829) was born in New York City and graduated from Kings College which is presently Columbia University. He was a distinguished member of the First Continental Congress and served for a brief period of time in the Second Continental Congress. Jay was a major force behind getting New York to ratify the *Constitution*. This patriot had the honor of being the first Chief Justice of the United States Supreme Court. He along with John Adams and Benjamin Franklin negotiated the treaty ending the war with England. On October 12, 1816, John Jay said this: *"It is the duty, as well as the privilege and interest of our Christian nation to select and prefer Christians for their rulers,"* Once, while in Paris, Jay was asked if he believed in Christ. His response was this: *"I answered that I did, and that I thanked God that I did."*

Mrs. Philip Livingston's Raccoon Pot Pie Recipe

Mrs. Livingston First Made Her Marinade Like This:

1 quart water	¼ tsp allspice
1 pint cider vinegar	½ tsp garlic, chopped fine
1 tbls salt	1 tbls onion, chopped fine
¼ tsp red pepper	1 tbls molasses
1 tsp black pepper	1 tbls brown sugar

Blend all of the above ingredients and put in a small stone pot. Set aside while preparing the meat.

Now skin the raccoon. Carefully cut out scent glands and discard. Trim off all excess fat from the meat. Cut raccoon into pieces. Place meat pieces in stone pot with marinade. Set aside in cool place and let soak overnight or longer until ready to cook.

When ready to prepare meat for a meal, remove from marinade and drain. Now fix the following:

2 large onions, diced	Flour to suit
4 potatoes, cut up	1 tbls butter
3 ears of corn, cut in thirds	Salt to suit taste
Pepper to suit taste	

Put pieces of raccoon meat in cooking pot and cover with water. Bring to a boil and let simmer until meat is tender. Add onions, potatoes and corn. When all vegetables are tender, take them and meat from broth in pot. Remove bones from meat and discard. Cut meat into small pieces. Slowly add flour enough to broth in pot until it thickens and makes a nice gravy. Stir in butter. Season to taste with salt and pepper. Place meat and vegetables in a baking pan and pour gravy over them. Now prepare dough covering for top of pot pie as follows:

2 cups flour	½ tsp salt
4 tsp baking powder	2 tbls shortening
¾ cup milk	

Sift together flour, baking powder and salt in a wooden mixing bowl. Add shortening and cut in thoroughly with a fork. Slowly stir in liquid and mix until soft dough is formed. Roll or pat out with hands on floured board to about ¾ inch thick. Cover ingredients in baking pan with this dough. Punch holes in dough with fork to allow steam to escape. Bake at 450 degrees until nicely browned. Serve while steaming hot.

** ** ** ** **

Philip Livingston (1716-78) was a heroic New York signer of the *Declaration of Independence*. This brave Christian patriot lost his two homes as well as most of his business property as a result of his unselfish devotion to the cause of freedom in his beloved America. He died soon thereafter while still separated from his family by the War for Independence. So strong were the convictions of Philip Livingston that he willingly risked everything he had in this life for the American Revolution -- for the freedom and liberty we have today in our great country.

George Mason's Favorite Pheasant Casserole Dish

2 pound pheasant, dressed
2 tsp salt
2 tbls butter
2 tbls flour
4 cups sauerkraut
3 tbls molasses or 3 tbls brown sugar
3 apples, cut in wedges
½ cup water
¾ tsp caraway seed
½ cup white wine

Rinse pheasant thoroughly inside and out. Drain well. Cut pheasant into small pieces and sprinkle with salt. Melt butter in cast iron skillet. Put in pheasant pieces and brown nicely on all sides. Take pheasant pieces from skillet and set aside to drain. Blend flour with drippings left remaining in skillet. Add sauerkraut and molasses or brown sugar. Blend thoroughly. Turn mixture into a baking pan of suitable size. Lay browned pheasant pieces on top of sauerkraut. Arrange apple wedges neatly around pheasant pieces. Add water. Cover and bake at 350 degrees for 1 hour. Uncover and sprinkle caraway seeds between pieces of pheasant. Lastly, pour wine between pheasant pieces so it seeps down into the sauerkraut. Again cover and bake 15 more minutes. Serve immediately. Makes enough to feed 4 to 6 people.

** ** ** ** **

George Mason (1725-92) was an early leader in the colonial cause of freedom. This patriot was a wealthy Virginia planter and close friend of George Washington. He was adamantly against the taxing policies of the British.

This devout Christian leader assisted in the development of the *Constitution*, but then strongly opposed its ratification in Virginia. Mason believed it gave the federal government too much power and, therefore, could take away the rights of the states as well as those of the citizens.

5

Turkey, Goose and Duck – Favorites of Our Forefathers

Mrs. Hopkins Special Creamed Turkey Dish

2 cups turkey, cooked	1 tbls onion, chopped fine
3 tbls butter	½ tsp salt
2 tbls flour	½ tsp pepper
1 cup turkey broth	½ cup cream
¼ cup celery, chopped fine	⅛ tsp mace

Remove all skin and gristle from turkey meat. Cut into ½ inch to ¾ cubes and set aside momentarily. Meanwhile, melt butter in large cast iron skillet. Stir in flour. Blend carefully so there are no lumps. Slowly add turkey broth and turkey meat. Next stir in chopped celery, onion, salt and pepper. Allow mixture to simmer for 10 minutes. Lastly stir in cream and mace. Heat everything thoroughly. Fill split popovers as made below and serve at once with buttered young peas. Makes enough to feed 4 people nicely.

Mrs. Hopkins Popovers

1 cup flour	2 eggs
¼ tsp salt	1 tbls shortening, melted
	1 cup milk

Sift together the flour and salt in a wooden mixing bowl. Make a well in flour and break eggs in well. Add melted shortening and milk. Stir until smooth. Pour into buttered gem pans. Bake at 350 degrees for 20 minutes. Increase heat to 450 degrees for 10 minutes. Reduce heat and allow to dry out for about 10 more minutes. Makes 10 popovers.

** ** ** ** **

Stephen Hopkins (1707-85) of Rhode Island, afflicted with palsy, was the second oldest signer of the *Declaration of Independence*. After this great Christian patriot affixed his signature to the document, he handed the quill to William Ellery. Hopkins spoke: ***"My hand trembles, but my heart does not."*** Hopkins was a man of unquestionable courage who never doubted the rightfulness of the quest for American independence from England. He stood tall and unwavering for freedom when it counted the most.

Baked Duck as Prepared in the Rodney Household

3 to 4 pound duck, dressed	2 garlic cloves, minced
2 tbls baking soda	1-½quarts sauerkraut
3 tsp salt	3 apples, chopped
½ cup butter	1 cup celery, diced
1 cup onions, chopped	1 tsp caraway seed

Take duck and rub baking soda thoroughly into skin. When finished, rinse duck well with warm water, both inside and out. Set aside to drain for a few minutes. Then carefully sprinkle both inside and out with salt. Set aside while the butter is being melted in a large cast iron skillet. Then stir in chopped onions and minced garlic. Sauté until onions turn light brown. Meanwhile, drain sauerkraut and set liquid aside. Add sauerkraut, apples, celery and caraway seeds to the onions and garlic in skillet. Blend thoroughly. Fill cavity of duck with this stuffing. Place duck in roasting pan. Arrange left over stuffing around duck. Bury giblets in left over stuffing. Cover and bake at 350 degrees for 2 hours. Then uncover and bake 1 hour longer to brown duck. Use sauerkraut liquid previously set aside to baste duck about every 30 minutes during roasting. Make gravy from drippings by adding flour as needed to thicken. Add salt and pepper to suit taste. Makes enough to feed 4 to 6 people.

** ** ** ** **

Caesar Rodney (1728-84), a signer of the *Declaration of Independence*, was the 47 year old son of a wealthy plantation owner. This dedicated Christian patriot covered his head with a green silk scarf to hide his terrible facial cancer. A colleague described him as: ***"An animated skeleton with a bandaged head."*** Yet, despite his deadly affliction, Rodney courageously rode all night through a rainstorm to be in Philadelphia in time to join with his fellow patriots in signing the historic declaration.

Roast Turkey with Cranberry Stuffing as Eaten by von Steuben

14 pound turkey, dressed   Salt as needed
Pepper as needed

Carefully wash turkey, inside and out, with cold water. Dry inside, but leave outside moist. Salt and pepper neck and body cavities liberally. Set turkey aside and prepare stuffing as follows:

1 cup butter	5 cups celery, diced
1 large onion, chopped	1-½ tbls salt
4 cups water	1 tsp poultry seasoning
3 cups cranberry juice	6 cups rice, cooked
½ cup cranberries, chopped	¾ cups parsley, chopped

Put butter in large cooking kettle and melt. Stir in chopped onion and let cook until tender and lightly browned. Add water, cranberry juice, chopped cranberries, diced celery, salt and poultry seasoning. Blend everything well and let come to a boil. Then stir in cooked rice. Take from fire, cover kettle and set aside to let stand 5 minutes. Then stir in parsley. Use fork to fluff up dressing. Now stuff turkey. Place turkey, breast up, on rack in roasting pan. Cover loosely. Bake at 325 degrees for 5 hours. Any extra stuffing can be put in roasting pan around turkey 30 minutes before turkey is done.

** ** ** ** **

General Frederick William Augustus Henry Ferdinand von Steuben (1730-94) was a fine, highly regarded Prussian military strategist. This great Christian patriot came to the colonies and volunteered his much needed services to the emerging nation during the Revolutionary War. He is best remembered for instilling discipline in the Continental Army at Valley Forge. General von Steuben was able to revive the disheartened troops and make them ready to fight the British. He took a major part in the Battle of Yorktown with General Washington. This great military leader must be given much of the credit for the defeat of the British in America's War for Independence.

Chicken and Oysters – An Adams Family Favorite

½ cup butter	½ cup flour
1 tsp salt	1 cup spinach, chopped
¼ tsp pepper	4 cups cooked chicken, diced
4 cups cream	1 quart oysters, drained
1 cup celery, chopped fine	

Put butter in cast iron skillet and melt. Add salt, pepper and cream. Blend well. Slowly stir in flour so as not to lump. Then add spinach and cooked chicken pieces. Mix everything thoroughly. Lastly add the oysters. Let mixture simmer until oysters are nice and plump. Sprinkle over nicely with finely chopped celery and serve immediately.

** ** ** ** **

John Adams (1735-1826) was the 2nd President of the United States who served his country in this position from 1797 to 1801. Adams, the first President to live in the White House, graduated from Harvard and considered going into the ministry at one time. He was elected to be vice-president under George Washington and was re-elected in 1792. This great American patriot was a member of the Continental Congress and a signer of the *Declaration of Independence*. He personally asked Thomas Jefferson to write the *Declaration of Independence* and he was the man who was most influential in getting George Washington appointed as Commander-in-Chief of the Continental Army. Expressing his Christian belief, Adams once said this: ***"And may that Being who is supreme over all   continue His blessings upon this nation."*** Regarding July 2, 1773, the day Congress approved the *Declaration of Independence*, Adams said that he believed this to be the most memorable period in America's history: ***"It ought to be commemorated,*** *as a Day of Deliverance, by solemn acts of devotion to God Almighty.* "

Roast Pheasant as Enjoyed by the Gates Family

2 to 3 pound pheasant, dressed	½ tsp poultry seasoning
¼ cup butter	½ tsp salt
½ cup celery, chopped fine	⅛ tsp pepper
½ cup onion, minced	3 tbls parsley, chopped
3 cups breadcrumbs	¾ cup milk
	¼ pound salt pork, sliced thin

Rinse pheasant inside and out with cold water and allow to drain thoroughly. Liberally salt neck and body cavity and set aside. Melt butter in large cast iron skillet. Stir in chopped celery and minced onion. Sauté for about 5 or 6 minutes until onion is soft and yellow in appearance. Now add bread crumbs, poultry seasoning, salt, pepper and chopped parsley. Toss with a spoon until everything is nicely blended. Slowly pour milk over this mixture while stirring with a fork. Pack into both neck and body cavity of pheasant. Place bird, breast up, on rack of roasting pan. Lay slices of salt pork over breast of pheasant and over each leg. Cover pan and roast at 350 degrees for 1-1/2 hour. Then take cover from roasting pan and cook for 30 minutes longer to brown nicely. Remove pan from oven and discard slices of salt pork. Serve pheasant while hot.

** ** ** ** **

General Horatio Gates (1728-1806), born in England, was a top officer in the Continental Army under the command of General George Washington. This prominent Christian military leader was instrumental in defeating the British at Saratoga, New York, on October 17, 1777, under the command of General Burgoyne. Three days after Burgoyne surrendered, Gates write to his wife: ***If old England is not by this lesson taught humility, then she is an obstinate old slut, bent upon her ruin.***

Baked Chicken as Prepared for the Bassett Family

2 chickens, cut up	4 eggs
Butter to suit	1 cup milk
Pepper to suit	1 cup flour
Salt to suit	1 tsp baking powder
1 tsp salt	

Put chicken pieces in large cooking pot, cover with water, and parboil. Meanwhile, butter a large baking pan and set aside until needed. When chicken pieces are ready, take from pot and let them cool. Then lay them in baking pan and dot each piece with small lump of butter. Sprinkle with pepper and salt. Now put eggs in a wooden mixing bowl and beat until light and frothy. Stir in the milk, flour, baking powder and salt. Blend all ingredients well. Pour this mixture over chicken pieces in baking pan. Put in oven and bake at 350 degrees for 1 hour. Serve while hot.

** ** ** ** **

Richard Bassett (1745-1815) is another man often forgotten in America's historical past. This man was converted to Methodism while serving in the Continental Army as a captain during the Revolutionary War. Bassett, a Delaware planter, attended the Constitutional Convention and was a signer of the *Constitution*. He was a major force behind getting his state to be the first to ratify this grand document. Described as *"a religious enthusiast"* by Major William Pierce of Georgia, another delegate to the Constitutional Convention, Bassett was a devout Christian. He went on to later become Governor of Delaware and also the Chief Justice of the Supreme Court of Delaware.

Mrs. Whipple's Stuffed Roast Goose

10 pound goose, dressed

Carefully wash goose, inside and out, with cold water. Dry inside thoroughly with a towel. Leave outside moist. Cut wings off at first joint. Cut neck into 1 inch sections. Set these aside for later use. Remove some of the fat from the cavity and put in a cast iron skillet. Fry over low heat. Leave about 3 tablespoons of this goose grease in skillet and prepare stuffing as follows:

1 cup onion, minced	4 cups bread crumbs
1 garlic clove, chopped fine	½ cup brandy
¾ pound chicken livers, chopped	2 eggs, beaten
Goose liver, chopped	1 tsp salt
2-½ cups apples, chopped	¼ tsp pepper

⅓ cup parsley, chopped

Put onion in skillet with goose grease and sauté for 3 minutes. Add garlic, chopped chicken livers and chopped goose liver. Stir while frying for 2 more minutes. Set aside until cool. When cooled, dump into large wooden mixing bowl. Add bread crumbs, chopped apple, brandy, beaten eggs. salt, pepper and parsley. Blend everything by tossing with large spoon.

Stuff goose with this mixture. Place goose, breast facing up, on rack of roasting pan. Bake at 425 degrees for 25 minutes. Now you will need the following:

1-¼ cups celery, chopped
2 cups onion, chopped
1-½ cups port wine
1-½ cups chicken broth
2 tsp cornstarch

Take goose from roasting pan. Pour off fat. Put chopped celery, onion, neck sections and wing tips in bottom of roasting pan. Place goose back on rack in pan. Return roasting pan to oven and bake at 350 degrees for 2-1/2 hours.

Lastly, take goose from pan and place on large platter. Put in a warm place. Pour fat from roasting pan into small pot. Add port wine, stir well, and bring mixture to a boil. Allow to simmer for 2 to 3 minutes. Stir in chicken broth. Let simmer for 3 more minutes. Then mix cornstarch with 1 teaspoon warm water. Stir this into the mixture. Continue simmering, stirring constantly, until mixture thickens. Pour gravy into sauceboat and serve with goose.

** ** ** ** **

Abraham Whipple (1733-1819) gained a great deal of fame as a top flight naval officer from Rhode Island during the American War for Independence. This great Christian leader eventually achieved the rank of Commodore and was the commander of two armed vessels. Whipple was instrumental in the capture of 26 French ships while on a single cruise. His name was known throughout the Colonies for his exploits as a privateer when he captured 10 British ships in 10 nights. The name of Abraham Whipple is often forgotten in our glorious history, but he was one of the true heroes of the American Revolutionary War period.

6

Savory Stuffings from Years Gone By

Giblet Stuffing as Made by Mrs. Lewis

Giblets
1 large onion, chopped fine
2 celery stalks, chopped
1 cup potato, cooked and diced
1 egg, slightly beaten
2 cups cracker crumbs
½ cup salt pork, diced
1 tsp sage
Salt to suit taste
Pepper to suit taste

Put giblets in a small cast iron kettle and cover with water. Cover and bring to a boil. Let simmer until tender. Take giblets from kettle. Set broth aside and save until later. Chop giblets into small pieces. Put into wooden mixing bowl and add chopped onion, celery, potato, beaten egg, cracker crumbs, salt pork and sage. Blend all ingredients thoroughly. Lastly season to taste with salt and pepper. Moisten with the broth from kettle in which giblets were cooked. Mixture should be soft enough to drop from a spoon. Arrange around turkey after it has been placed in the roasting pan.

** ** ** ** **

Francis Lewis (1713-1802), a signer of the *Declaration of Independence* from New York, was away when the British, well known for their unwarranted brutality during the Revolutionary War period, made a surprise reprisal raid on his home. They ransacked the place, destroying everything. The British soldiers severely beat his wife and then took her away and threw her in prison. She died a short time after she was finally released in a prisoner exchange in 1778. Lewis was another of the heroic signers who paid dearly for his beliefs in liberty and freedom. Yet through all the trials and tribulations, this great Christian patriot never wavered.

Mushroom Stuffing for Roast Chicken – an Aaron Burr Favorite

½ cup butter
1 cup mushrooms,
    chopped
2 tbls onion,
    minced
4 tbls celery,
    diced fine

6 cups bread,
    stale and cubed
1 tsp salt
¼ tsp pepper
1 cup broth (made
    from giblets and neck)
2 eggs, beaten

Melt butter in a large cast iron skillet. Add mushrooms and onion. Stir well and cover. Let simmer 4 to 5 minutes until onions are soft and mushrooms are covered with their own juice. Set aside to cool. Then add diced celery, bread cubes, salt and pepper. Mix nicely with large spoon. Combine broth and beaten eggs in wooden mixing bowl and stir. Pour this over mixture in skillet and blend thoroughly. Pack lightly in cavity of chicken. Makes enough stuffing for a 3 pound chicken.

** ** ** ** **

Aaron Burr (1756-1836) served with distinction in the Continental Army during the American War for Independence. He was later vice-president of the United

States under President Thomas Jefferson from 1801 to 1805. A professed Christian, this man gained lasting historical notoriety when he mortally wounded Alexander Hamilton in a duel. He was later charged with treason but was finally cleared of this. Nevertheless, Burr fled the United States and lived in Europe for a number of years.

Mrs. Pinckney's Best Oyster Stuffing as Made for Her Son Charles

12 slices stale bread	1 pint oysters
½ cup butter	2 tsp poultry seasoning
3 onions, minced	1 egg, well beaten
1 cup celery, chopped	Salt to suit taste
1 cup parsley, chopped	Pepper to suit taste

Trim crust from bread slices. Cut slices into small cubes and set aside. Put butter in large cast iron skillet and melt. Add oysters, onions, celery and parsley. Stir well and let simmer for 8 to 10 minutes. Then stir in bread cubes, poultry seasoning and beaten egg. Add salt and pepper to suit taste. Toss lightly with large spoon until everything is nicely moistened and blended. Makes about 10 cups of poultry stuffing.

** ** ** ** **

Charles Pinckney (1757-1824) was another member of the prominent Charleston, South Carolina, family who played such an important role in formulating and then ratifying the *United States Constitution*. He also served with distinction in the Continental Army as did Charles Cotesworth Pinckney and Thomas Pinckney. This great Christian leader was captured by the British when Charleston fell and was held prisoner until the end of the war. He later served as a delegate to the Constitutional Convention where he played a very important role. Charles then later served several terms as Governor of South Carolina.

Bacon-Chestnut Stuffing – A Morton Family Treasure

1 pound bacon, diced	1 tsp thyme
¼ pound ham, diced	1 tsp sage
⅓ cup parsley, chopped	1-¼ tsp salt
¾ cup celery, chopped	½ tsp pepper
1 cup onion, minced	2 quarts bread crumbs, stale

1 pound chestnuts, cooked and chopped

Put bacon and ham in large cast iron skillet and fry until lightly browned. Add chopped parsley, celery, onion, thyme, sage, salt and pepper. Blend all these ingredients well and let simmer in skillet with bacon and ham for about 6 minutes. Meanwhile, put bread crumbs and chestnuts in a large wooden mixing bowl. Pour mixture from skillet over bread crumbs and chestnuts. Toss lightly with large spoon until everything is nicely moistened and thoroughly blended. Makes about 10 cups of poultry stuffing.

** ** ** ** **

John Morton (1725-77) of Pennsylvania was another heroic signer of the *Declaration of Independence* who paid dearly for his unfaltering belief in and love for the great American cause. This staunch, *Bible* believing Christian, was rejected by his family and friends for his dedication to liberty and freedom. Morton said these final words on his death bed: ***"Tell them that they will live to see the hour when they shall acknowledge it [the signing] to have been the most glorious service that I ever rendered to my country."*** Yes, even to taking his last breath, John Morton never doubted that he had done the right thing. He never wavered in his convictions.

The Trumbull Family's Best Giblet Stuffing
for Duck and Pheasant

¼ cup butter
½ cup onion,
    chopped
3 tbls celery,
    chopped
2 tbls green bell pepper,
    chopped

1 garlic clove,
    minced
½ tsp salt
¼ tsp pepper
Giblets and neck meat,
    cooked and chopped
3 cups bread crumbs

Cream to suit

Melt butter in a large cast iron skillet. Add onion and sauté lightly until they turn light brown. Then stir in celery, green pepper, salt and pepper. Add cooked giblets and neck meat. Blend everything well. Now put bread crumbs in skillet. Pour cream over crumbs, and using a large spoon, toss lightly until everything is nicely moistened. Stuff lightly into cavity of duck or pheasant. Makes enough stuffing to pack a 2 pound duck or pheasant. Double this recipe for a 3 to 4 pound chicken.

** ** ** ** **

Jonathan Trumbull (1710-85) was a true Christian patriot in every sense of the word. A braver man would be difficult to find in American history. He was the British Governor of Connecticut who had been appointed by King George 111, but he was openly sympathetic to the American cause. Trumbull was the only Colonial Governor who boldly dared to refuse to take the oath required by the British government for all officers of the Crown. On July 13, 1775, he wrote to General Washington letting him know of his support for him as head of the Continental Army. And in August of 1776, in response to Washington's desperate plea for reinforcements, Jonathan Trumbull came through with nine regiments of volunteers for the Continental Army. His appeal for those much needed volunteers read in part: *"May the Lord of Hosts, the God of the armies of Israel, be your Captain, your Leader, your Conductor, and Saviour."*

Onion-Celery Stuffing as Made by the Paine Family

¼ cup butter	1 tsp thyme
1 garlic clove, minced	1 tsp salt
2 cups onion, chopped	¼ tsp pepper
2 cups celery, chopped	¾ cup turkey broth
1 tsp sage	4 cups bread crumbs, stale

Melt butter in a large cast iron skillet or kettle. Stir in minced garlic, chopped onion and celery, sage, thyme, salt and pepper. Allow to simmer 6 to 8 minutes. Then add turkey broth and bread crumbs. Mix thoroughly. Toss lightly with large spoon until everything is moist and nicely blended. Makes about 5 cups of poultry stuffing.

** ** ** ** **

Thomas Paine (1737-1809) fanned the flames of Colonial independence with his December 23, 1776, essay, *"The American Crisis."* General George Washington was so inspired by this essay that he ordered it be read aloud to the Colonial Army at Valley Forge. In it, Paine wrote: *"Tyranny, like hell, is not easily conquered; yet we have this consolation with us, that the harder the conflict, the more glorious the triumph. ... The cause of America is the cause of all mankind. Where, say some, is the king of America? I'll tell you, friend, He reigns above."* Thomas Paine called himself an *"Englishman by birth, French citizen by decree, and American by adoption."* His last words before he died were: *"I die in perfect composure and resignation to the will of my Creator, God."*

Mrs. Randolph's Special Walnut Crème Stuffing

3 quarts bread crumbs	3 fresh sage leaves, chopped
2 cups butter	2 cups heavy cream
1-½ pounds walnuts broken up	Salt to suit taste
	Pepper to suit taste

Spread bread crumbs out on a baking tin and dry thoroughly in oven. Meanwhile put ¼ cup of the butter in cast iron skillet and melt. When melted, add walnut pieces and allow to simmer until lightly browned. Remove walnut pieces and put into large wooden mixing bowl and set aside. Put the rest of the butter in the skillet and melt. Add dried bread crumbs and cook until browned. Now add bread crumbs and chopped sage leaves to nuts in mixing bowl. Stir well to mix. Add heavy cream and work in with hands until everything is moistened thoroughly. Salt and pepper to taste. Makes about 12 cups of turkey stuffing, or a delightful stuffing for any other poultry dish.

** ** ** ** **

Edmund Jennings Randolph (1753-1813), a Virginian, served in the Continental Army under General George Washington during the American War for Independence.

This devout Christian patriot was later a member of the Continental Congress and was a delegate to the Constitutional Convention. Randolph proposed that every session of Congress be opened each morning with prayer. He also served his country as its first Attorney General and its second Secretary of State. This great patriot also played a major role in forging the *Constitution*, yet he refused to sign it and initially opposed its adoption. However, he later greatly assisted in getting this historic document ratified in Virginia.

7

Meat Cookery During the War for Independence

Mrs. Carroll's Favorite Liver Loaf Dish

1 pound liver	1 egg, beaten
1 onion, large	1 cup milk
1 cup bread crumbs	1 tsp salt

Put liver in kettle and cover with salted water. Bring to boil and let cook for 10 minutes. Then grind together with onion in food grinder. Put in large wooden mixing bowl with bread crumbs, beaten egg, milk and salt. Blend ingredients thoroughly. Dump into well greased loaf pan. Set pan in larger baking pan of hot water. Bake at 350 degrees for 30 minutes. Serve while hot.

** ** ** ** **

Charles Carroll (1737-1832), American patriot and legislator from Maryland, was a direct descendant of Irish kings. He was the only man to sign the *Declaration of*

Independence who was a Roman Catholic. Carroll was known to be one of the wealthiest man in the Colonies during the Revolutionary War period of our history. He returned in 1800 to his 10,000 acre Carrollton Manor. This man outlived all the other signers of the *Declaration* and died at the age of 95.

Stuffed Flank Steak as Eaten by Noah Webster

1 cup crackers, coarsely broken	¼ tsp salt
1 cup oats, cooked	⅛ tsp pepper
3 tbls onion, chopped	½ tsp sage
1 tbls parsley, chopped	1 large flank steak
4 tbls bacon grease	1 cup hot water

4 slices bacon

Put crackers, oats, onion, parsley, 2 tablespoons bacon grease, salt, pepper and sage in wooden mixing bowl. Stir until all ingredients are nicely blended. Spread evenly over flank steak. Carefully roll steak up lengthwise and fasten with skewer. Fry in large cast iron skillet in other 2 tablespoons bacon grease until nicely browned on all sides. Then place in baking pan. Add water. Lay bacon slices across top. Bake at 350 degrees for 3 hours. When done, slice into six even portions and serve.

** ** ** ** **

Noah Webster (1758-1843) was a patriot and believer in the great American cause. He served honorably as a soldier during the Revolutionary War. This great Christian was the one person most responsible for Article 1, Section 8, of the

81

United States Constitution. He became best known as the author of *"Webster's Dictionary."* Webster's *"American Spelling Book,"* first written in the 1780s, set a record in the publishing field as it sold more then a million copies each year for more than 100 years. Noah Webster clearly expressed his beliefs when he made these statements: *"Education is useless without the Bible. ... The Bible was America's basic text book in all fields. ... God's Word, contained in the Bible, has furnished all necessary rules to direct our conduct."*

Roast Beaver as Prepared by Silas Deane

1 beaver, dressed	2 large onions, sliced
Baking soda to suit	3 cloves garlic, crushed
Salt to suit	½ pound bacon, sliced

Trim fat off meat and discard. Put meat in cast iron kettle. Cover with mixture of baking soda and water. Put 1 teaspoon baking soda for every quart of water used. Bring to boil and then allow to simmer for 10 to 15 minutes. Take meat from kettle and drain well. Put into roasting pan. Sprinkle with salt. Cover with sliced onions. Then lay strips of bacon over onions. Cover and bake at 350 degrees until meat is so well done it falls from bones. Serve immediately.

** ** ** ** **

Silas Deane (1737-89) was a delegate to the Continental Congress from 1794 to 1796. This devout Christian was extremely important to the patriot cause during the Revolutionary War. His diplomatic service in France was instrumental in successfully obtaining much needed supplies early in the war. Deane worked tirelessly for the cause of freedom in America but he was recalled to face serious charges before Congress over his financial dealings. Although never proven to be dishonest, a cloud of suspicion followed him the rest of his life.

How George Rogers Clark Fixed His Possum

2 to 3 pound possum, dressed
2 tbls salt
2 tsp pepper
1 cup flour

6 sweet potatoes,
   quartered
3 tbls brown sugar
1 cup water

Put possum on ice and thoroughly chill. Then trim off fat and discard. Carefully wash possum, inside and out, with warm water. Drain well. Blend together salt and pepper. Rub this mixture all over possum, both inside and out. Then sprinkle flour all over possum. Lay possum face up in roasting pan. Add water and cover tightly. Bake at 350 degrees for 1 hour. Take from oven, uncover, and lay sweet potato quarters around possum. Add more water as needed. Cover and bake 30 more minutes. Again remove from oven, uncover, and sprinkle brown sugar on sweet potato pieces. Put back in oven, this time uncovered. Continue baking until everything is nicely browned.

** ** ** ** **

George Rogers Clark (1752-1818) was a renowned military leader on the American frontier. This man moved to Kentucky in 1775 and organized the militia there during the Revolutionary War. He began attacking British outposts in Illinois with less than 200 men. An unwavering Christian leader, Clark's successes there brought the French inhabitants in the area to his side in the war. After British General Henry Hamilton occupied Vincennes in December of 1778, Clark counter-attacked with a small group during the harsh winter in February of 1779. Marching for 18 days through icy water, often with little or no food, his men defeated the British and took General Hamilton prisoner. Hamilton later said that Clark's military feat was *"unequaled perhaps in history."*

Mrs. Witherspoon's Best Squirrel and Gravy Dish

2 squirrels, dressed	½ cup butter
3 tsp salt	¾ cup water
1 tsp pepper	1-½ cups milk
1 cup flour	1 tsp onion, grated

Wash squirrels thoroughly, inside and out, with warm water. Drain well. Cut up into serving size pieces and set aside momentarily. Meanwhile combine salt, pepper and flour in small wooden mixing bowl. Melt butter in large cast iron skillet. Dredge squirrel pieces in flour mixture and then place in skillet. Fry slowly until nicely browned on all sides. Then add ¼ cup of the water. Cover skillet tightly. Reduce heat. Let simmer for 30 minutes. Add rest of water as needed. Squirrel meat should be extremely tender when it is done. Put meat pieces on hot platter and cover to keep warm. Put leftover flour in skillet with liquid left from cooking. Gradually add milk. Stir in grated onion. Bring mixture to a boil while stirring constantly. When gravy thickens, serve at once with squirrel pieces.

** ** ** ** **

John Witherspoon (1723-94), a Scotsman, had the distinction of being the only clergyman to sign the *Declaration of Independence*. Witherspoon was a dignified, persuasive man of Calvinist austerity. A member of the Continental Congress, he served on more than 100 Congressional Committees. Witherspoon was widely known early on as a Revolutionary patriot. Sadly, he lost two of his sons in the War for American Independence. When this great man died, John Adams, one of his multitude of admirers called him *"a true son of liberty. So he was. But first, he was a son of the Cross."*

Simple Meat Souffle – A Madison Household Favorite

6 tbls flour	¼ tsp pepper
4 tbls butter, melted 1-	½ cup beef, chopped fine
1 cup milk, scalded	6 egg yolks, well beaten
1 tsp salt	6 egg whites, beaten stiff

Combine the flour, melted butter, scalded milk, salt and pepper in a small cooking pot. Stir continuously while cooking over hot water until it thickens and is smooth and lump free. Then stir in chopped beef and remove from stove. Continue stirring until everything is thoroughly blended. Now stir in beaten egg yolks. Set aside to cool. When cooled, fold in the stiffly beaten egg whites. Pour mixture into well buttered casserole dish or baking pan. Place in larger pan of warm water. Bake at 375 degrees for 20 minutes. Check for doneness by inserting knife into souffle. It is done when knife comes out clean. Serve immediately while hot. Makes enough to serve 12 people.

** ** ** ** **

James Madison (1751-1836) was Secretary of State under Thomas Jefferson as well as the 4th President of the United States from 1809 to 1817. He was a leading member of the Continental Congress. Madison's most important contribution as one of our great Forefathers was his work in formulating our *Constitution*. He is often credited by historians as being the *"Father of the Constitution."* This title is no doubt more deservingly given to him than to any other single individual. Madison, more than any other patriot leader of his time, pushed the *Bill of Rights* through Congress. A devout Christian, he once said: *"We have staked the whole future of American civilization upon the capacity of mankind … to sustain ourselves according to the Ten Commandments of God."*

Lamb Mousse as Served by Mrs. Wythe

3 egg yolks, slightly beaten   1 tbls gelatin
¼ tsp salt   1 cup lamb, cooked
¼ tsp paprika   and ground fine
1 cup lamb broth   1 tbls cayenne
1 cup cream, stiffly beaten

Combine egg yolks, salt and paprika in large cast iron skillet and stir to mix nicely. Add lamb broth slowly while constantly stirring. Cook until mixture begins to thicken. Soften gelatin in 1 tablespoon cold water. Add this to skillet and stir until dissolved. Now add ground lamb. Season with cayenne pepper. Take skillet from stove and set mixture aside to cool. Then chill until it thickens. Fold in fluffy whipped cream. Pour mixture from skillet into ring mold and chill on ice until firm. Unmold. Fill center with marinated shredded cabbage and carrot mixture. Serve on platter.

** ** ** ** **

George Wythe (1726-1806) from Virginia, was one of the 56 heroic signers of the *Declaration of Independence*. He was also a member of the Continental Congress. Wythe established the first law professorship in the United States at

William and Mary College and taught such great patriots as Thomas Jefferson, Henry Clay and John Marshall. This man freed his slaves in his will and left his entire library to Jefferson. He died before his time due to arsenic poisoning by a greedy grand nephew who was impatiently waiting for his inheritance. In February of 1776, Wythe, a devout Christian, helped John Adams and Robert Sherman write up instructions for an embassy to be opened in Canada: *"You are further to declare ... that ... the right to hold office was to be extended to persons of any Christian denomination."*

8

Dessert Specials from the Olden Days

Apple-Ale Fritters as Cooked for George Washington

2 cups strong ale	1 tsp nutmeg
¼ cup white wine	½ tsp cloves
3 egg yolks, well beaten	½ tsp mace
2 egg whites, well beaten	Sugar as needed
Flour to suit	Cinnamon as needed

8 apples, cut in small chunks

Blend the ale and wine in a cast iron skillet and heat until slightly warmed. Meanwhile, combine in a large wooden mixing bowl the beaten egg yolks, beaten egg whites and enough flour to make a very thick batter. Beat these ingredients thoroughly and then stir in the warm ale-wine mixture. Add nutmeg, cloves and mace and blend in. Lastly, drop apple pieces into batter, stir well, and set aside until kettle of cooking grease is heated. When grease is hot enough for deep frying, drop batter in by large spoonfuls and fry until nicely browned. Then remove each fritter from kettle and lay on clean cloth or paper to drain. Serve while hot. Sprinkle with cinnamon and sugar just before serving.

Note: *Do not use any more flour once ale-egg mixture has been added to this recipe. Finished batter should be just thick enough to cling nicely to the apple pieces. This recipe for delicious apple-ale fritters comes from Frances Parke Custis, the mother-in-law of Martha Washington (mother of Martha's first husband, Daniel Custis). It was handed down in the family and subsequently prepared for her husband, George.*

** ** ** ** **

George Washington (1732-99) was the first President of the United States who served his country in this position from 1789 to 1797. He had also been selected in 1775 to be Commander-in-Chief of the Continental Army. This great American also holds the distinction of being chosen by his peers to be Chairman of the Constitutional Convention. Washington, a brilliant man, was never formally taught school beyond the elementary level. He was a surveyor by trade and served under General Braddock prior to the French and Indian War. He emerged later with a reputation as a great military leader. George Washington became the most popular individual in the Colonies and the most respected man among his peers. As to this man's Christian beliefs, he once said: ***"It is impossible to rightly govern the world without God and the Bible."***

Walnut Bread Pudding as Served to General Lafayette

1 cup sugar	1 tbls vanilla extract
4 large eggs	6 cups bread cubes, stale
3 cups milk	2 cups walnuts, broken up

Put sugar and eggs in small wooden mixing bowl and beat together 3 to 4 minutes or until light and fluffy. Then pour in milk and vanilla extract and again beat until thoroughly blended. Put bread cubes in large wooden mixing bowl. Pour first mixture over bread cubes and allow to soak for at least 30 minutes. Add broken walnut pieces and stir in with large mixing spoon. Preheat oven to 350 degrees. Meanwhile, butter an 8 x 10 x 2 inch baking pan. Pack bread pudding mixture in baking pan. Bake for 1 hour. Bread pudding, when finished baking, should look puffy and browned.

Now Prepare the Coffee-Crème Sauce

1 cup heavy cream	1 cup dark roast coffee
½ cup sugar	2 tbls corn starch
1 tbls water	

Combine heavy cream, sugar and dark roast coffee in small cooking kettle. Heat slowly. Now combine corn starch and water in small bowl or cup. Stir until corn starch is completely dissolved. Then whip this into the heated mixture in kettle. Continue until thickened. Pour this over individual servings of bread pudding. Makes enough to serve 15 people.

** ** ** ** **

Marquis de Lafayette ((1757-1834) was a devout Christian Frenchman who quickly proved his mettle on the battlefield. When he saw the American soldier's plight at Valley Forge he was horrified and wrote: *"They had neither coats, hats, shirts, nor shoes; their feet and legs froze until they became black. ... "* As we all know, this gallant young aristocrat had come from France to fight and shed his blood, if need be, at the side of General George Washington during America's War for Independence. The above **Walnut Bread Pudding** was actually served to this great patriot by my great-great grandmother Huldah Horton. Lafayette had dinner at her home in Newburg, New York, during his last visit to America in 1824.

The Walton Family's Blueberry Roly Polys

1-½ cups flour	1-½ cups milk
5 tsp baking powder	¼ cup molasses
1 tsp salt	¾ cup sugar
¼ tsp baking soda	1 tbls butter, melted
1-½ cups graham flour	1 cup blueberries

Sift together the flour, baking powder, salt and baking soda in a wooden mixing bowl. Then stir in graham flour and blend well. Mix together in another wooden mixing bowl the milk, molasses and ½ cup of the sugar. Add this to dry ingredients in first bowl and blend well. Add melted butter and mix in thoroughly. Roll out on floured board into an oblong piece about ½ inch thick. Sprinkle with blueberries and other ¼ cup sugar. Roll up dough to make large roll. Bake in greased shallow pan at 375 degrees for about 45 minutes. Slice and serve warm with pudding sauce or vanilla ice cream. **Note:** *The Walton family also enjoyed these Roly Polys when made with fresh blackberries, raspberries, strawberries and other fruits.*

** ** ** ** **

George Walton (1740-1804) of Georgia, largely forgotten today with the passage of time, was one of the 56 great men who affixed their names to the historic *Declaration of Independence*. He and the others all knew that, in the eyes of the British at least, they were committing an act of high treason against the Crown. Each signer knew the penalty for doing this was death by hanging should the Americans lose the war to the British. But, George Walton heroically signed the document despite the inherent dangers it presented. He was but one of many unwavering Christian patriots who bravely stood tall for freedom on that historic day in American history.

Pumpkin Custard – A Pickering Family Favorite

1 cup pumpkin, cooked
3 eggs, well beaten
¾ cup brown sugar
½ tsp salt

Pinch of nutmeg
½ tsp cinnamon
2 cups milk, scalding
1 cup cream

Put cooked pumpkin in large wooden mixing bowl and mash thoroughly. Blend in the frothy well beaten eggs, brown sugar, salt, nutmeg and cinnamon. Stir in scalding hot milk and beat hard. Now butter a quart baking pan and put mixture into it. Set baking pan in larger shallow pan of hot water. Place in oven and bake at 375 degrees for 25 to 30 minutes or until firm. When done, set aside to cool. When completely cooled, beat cup of cream until thick and fluffy. Serve custard with whipped cream on top.

** ** ** ** **

Colonel Timothy Pickering (1745-1829) gained fame during the American War for Independence. He heroically led his men in the first armed resistance against the British in February of 1775 at a drawbridge in Salem. Pickering, a fearless Christian officer, with a regiment of 700 loyal followers, later joined forces under the command of General

George Washington in New Jersey during the Fall of 1776. A Harvard graduate, Pickering was the man who planned the West Point military Academy. He later served as President Washington's Postmaster General, Secretary of War and Secretary of State.

Pumpkin Pie with Cheese Crust – A Specialty of the Sampson Family

½ cup raisins   ¼ tsp nutmeg
¼ tsp cinnamon   ¼ tsp salt
1 cup cream   2 eggs, slightly beaten
1 cup sugar   1 tbls butter
          1-½ cups fresh pumpkin, cooked

Combine all of the above ingredients in a large wooden mixing bowl and thoroughly blend. Set aside and make the crust as follows:

¾ cup flour   3 tbls butter
½ tsp salt   1-½ cups cheese, grated
          2 tbls cold water

Sift together the flour and salt in wooden mixing bowl. Cut in butter with fork until mixture is crumbly. Then stir in grated cheese. Blend thoroughly. Work water in lightly with spatula until little balls of dough just hang together in one large ball. Turn dough onto lightly floured board. Roll out in sheet 1/8 inch thick. Shape pastry dough to fit pie pan. Now pour pumpkin filling from mixing bowl into pastry-lined baking pan. Put in oven and bake at 425 degrees for about 25 minutes, or until inserted knife comes out clean.

** ** ** ** **

Deborah Sampson (1760-1827) was the first American woman who is known to have impersonated a man during the Revolutionary War in order to fight for her country. Yes, this 5'-7" woman joined the Continental Army's Massachusetts Regiment under the name of Robert Shurtleff on May 20, 1782. Although a devout Christian young lady,

Sampson was excommunicated from the First Baptist Church of Middleborough, Massachusetts, because of rumors circulating that she was *"dressing in men's clothing and enlisting as a soldier in the army."* Deborah was wounded in a leg at Tarrytown but took care of herself so no one would discover she was a woman. However, she was later hospitalized in Philadelphia with a fever and a doctor uncovered her secret. He quietly made arrangements for her to be honorably discharged from the military on October 25, 1783, by General Henry Knox. Deborah went on back home, married Benjamin Gannett, bore him three children and taught school. A special Act of Congress finally awarded her children compensation *"for the relief of the heirs of Deborah Gannet, a soldier of the Revolution."*

Mrs. Prescott's Old Fashioned Strawberry Shortcake

2 cups flour	2 tbls sugar
4 tsp baking powder	4 tbls butter
½ tsp salt	¾ cup milk

1 quart strawberries, crushed and sweetened

Sift together in a wooden mixing bowl the flour, baking powder, salt and sugar. Add butter and cut in with a fork until mixture is crumbly. Work in milk to make soft dough. Turn out dough onto floured board. Toss lightly until outside looks smooth. Divide dough into 2 equal halves. Shape into 2 rounds to fit layer cake pan. Place one round of dough in well-buttered cake pan. Spread over top of dough with soft butter. Place other dough round on top of first round. Bake at 400 degrees for about 25 minutes. Split while hot and butter top of both. Lastly spread crushed strawberries between and on top of layers. Serve with or without whipped cream. Serves 8 people.

** ** ** ** **

William Prescott (1726-95) is another often forgotten Christian patriot who believed fervently in the cause of American freedom. This great warrior was a Colonel during the Revolutionary War. He is best remembered for heroically commanding the Colonial Militia at the never-to-be-forgotten Battle of Bunker Hill. When the British brazenly blockaded the Boston port in 1774, Prescott wrote this in support of the people: *"Let us all be of one heart, and stand fast in the liberty wherewith Christ has made us free. And may He, of His infinite mercy, grant us deliverance from all our troubles."*

Dessert Sauces as Made by the Morris Family

Hard Sauce

⅓ cup butter   ¼ cup white wine
1 cup powdered sugar   Nutmeg

Cream the butter in small mixing bowl. Then add powdered sugar slowly, beating constantly. Add wine, a few drops at a time, and beat well. Sprinkle top with grated nutmeg just before serving.

Snowy Sauce

½ cup butter   Pinch of salt
1 cup powdered sugar   ½ tsp nutmeg

Cream the butter is small mixing bowl. Sift sugar and slowly add to creamed butter in bowl. Beat constantly. Add salt. Continue beating until smooth and fluffy. Pile in serving dish. Sprinkle with nutmeg. Chill.

** ** ** ** **

Robert Morris (1734-1806) of Pennsylvania was a wealthy man who became known as the *"financier of the American Revolution."* This devout Christian was a member of the Constitutional Convention in 1776. Prior to this, he was one of the 56 brave men who had the courage to take a stand for liberty and freedom and sign the *Declaration of Independence*. He and the other s clearly understood that they were pledging *"to each other our lives, our fortunes, and our sacred honor."*

9

Old-Timey Fruit Spreads

Spiced Jelly – A Braxton Family Favorite

1 peck grapes	2 tbls whole cloves
1 quart vinegar	2 tbls stick cinnamon, broken
6 pounds sugar	

Put grapes, vinegar, cloves and cinnamon in large kettle and heat slowly. Allow to cook until grapes are soft and mushy. Strain everything in kettle through double thickness of cheesecloth. Boil strained juice for 20 minutes while constantly stirring. Lastly, blend in sugar. Allow to boil 5 more minutes. Skim a little off top and test in this manner: put a teaspoonful on a saucer. Set in cool place for 1 minute. Scrape with spoon. If liquid on saucer did not begin to jell during this test, boil liquid in kettle a little longer. If surface has partly jelled, immediately pour mixture in kettle into glasses that have been rolled in hot water. Fill each glass to ½ inch from top. Let filled glasses stand for 24 hours in sunny window. After this, when jelly has stiffened, seal tops with covering of hot melted paraffin wax.

** ** ** ** **

Carter Braxton (1736-97) is another great American who is often forgotten with the passage of time. This man, a wealthy planter and trader from Virginia, bravely signed the *Declaration of Independence* despite the fact that he stood to lose everything for doing so. He knew full well the danger of his act. His reward? His fleet of ships was utterly destroyed by the British in retaliation. Braxton ended up selling all of his property to pay off his debts and he died a pauper. Yes, this great Christian patriot never wavered in his beliefs. He willingly gave his all for liberty and freedom when it counted the most.

Peach Preserves as Made for the Duche Thanksgiving Table

6 pounds peaches   9 cups sugar
1-½ cups water

Remove skins from peaches. Cut them open and throw away the pits. Cut peaches into 10 to 12 pieces each and set aside in a large wooden mixing bowl. Mix sugar and water in a large kettle and bring to boil. Allow to boil for 5 minutes. Toss in the peach pieces. Stir constantly while allowing to simmer until liquid thickens nicely. Spoon thickened mixture into sterilized jars or glasses. Fill jars to about ½ inch from top. Set aside to cool. When cold, seal tops with covering of hot melted paraffin wax.

** ** ** ** **

Jacob Duche (1738-98) was an Anglican clergyman. On September 6, 1774, the Continental Congress received shocking news! British troops had entered Boston! It was immediately decided that the first official act of Congress the very next morning would be to open with prayer. Reverend Duche was given the honor of leading this prayer in Carpenter's Hall, Philadelphia, extemporaneously, on September 7, 1774, at 9:00 a.m.

Apple Butter as Served to the Rush Family on Special Occasions

10 pounds tart apples	¼ tsp salt
1 quart cider	1-½ large cinnamon sticks
2-½ cups sugar	1-½ tsp anise seeds

Pare skin from apples, quarter them and remove core. Cut into thin slices. Put apple slices in large kettle. Add cider and allow to simmer until a nice sauce is obtained. Pour sauce into roasting pan. Cook in oven at 325 degrees for 1 hour or until sauce is reduced to ½ its original quantity. Stir occasionally while sauce is cooking in oven. Then blend in sugar and salt. Cook another hour while stirring much more frequently to prevent sticking or burning. Mixture should become a rich amber color. Lastly, put cinnamon sticks and anise seeds in loose cheesecloth bag. Add this to the apple butter in the roasting pan. Cook together for 30 more minutes. When done, remove spice bag and discard. Spoon hot apple butter mixture into sterilized jars or glasses. Fill each to about ½ from top. Set aside to cool. When cold, seal tops with covering of hot melted paraffin wax.

** ** ** ** **

Dr. Benjamin Rush (1745-1813) from Pennsylvania, was a signer of the *Declaration of Independence*. He served as Surgeon General of the Continental Army. Rush resigned after a disagreement with General Washington in 1777. After the War for American Independence ended, he set up the first free medical clinic in America. This man became the most famous physician and medical teacher in the country. In describing himself, this devout Christian said: *"I have alternately been called an Aristocrat and a Democrat. I am neither, I am a Christocrat."* Rush wrote to his wife during his final illness: *" ... blessed Jesus, wash away all my impurities, and receive me into Thy everlasting kingdom."*

Mrs. Ellery's Special Venison Jelly

8 quarts wild grapes   ¼ cup stick cinnamon, broken up
1 quart vinegar   ¼ cup cloves, whole
6 pounds sugar

Put grapes and vinegar in a large preserving kettle and stir well. Add cinnamon and cloves. Bring to quick boil. Then allow mixture to simmer until grapes are soft and mushy. Remove grapes and spices from kettle. Strain juice back into kettle through a jelly bag or double thickness of cheesecloth. Again bring to boil and continue boiling while stirring for 20 minutes. Stir in sugar. Boil 5 more minutes. Spoon out into sterilized glasses or jars. Fill each to about ½ inch from top. Set aside to cool. When cold, seal tops with covering of hot melted paraffin wax.

** ** ** ** **

William Ellery (1727-1820) of Rhode Island was another brave signer of the *Declaration of Independence*. He deliberately stood close to the table where each man came forward to sign the historic document. This unwavering Christian hero said that he wanted *"to see how they all looked as they signed what might be their death warrants."* Yes, each of these 56 men would have been hanged had the British won the war. During the occupation of Rhode Island by the British, Ellery suffered disastrous losses of his property. But he bore all this with a quiet cheerfulness as a sacrifice for the public good.

A Specialty of the Hopkinson Family – Pumpkin Butter

2 cups pumpkin, cooked   ½ tsp nutmeg
1 cup molasses   ½ tsp allspice
           1 tsp cinnamon

Put pumpkin, molasses, nutmeg, allspice and cinnamon in a small cast iron pot and blend well together. Allow to simmer, stirring continuously, until mixture thickens and becomes a buttery-like spread. Spoon out into a jar and set aside to cool before using. **Note:** *Mrs. Hopkinson also made special butters for her family by using sweet potatoes and squash instead of pumpkin. She sometimes substituted honey or maple syrup in place of molasses as her sweetener.*

** ** ** ** **

Francis Hopkinson (1737-91) was a signer of the *Declaration of Independence* from New Jersey. This great Christian patriot was also a notable poet and a talented song writer as well as an inventor in his day. He and Benjamin Franklin were close friends for many years. Hopkinson is credited with designing the Stars and Stripes in 1777. John Adams cold blue eyes took the measure of all those in

108

attendance at the signing of the *Declaration.* He characterized Hopkinson as having a head *"not bigger that a large apple."*

Peach Marmalade as Enjoyed by Fisher Ames

30 peaches   6 oranges
4 pounds sugar

Peel all peaches, remove pits and discard. Cut peaches into thin slices and put into stone crock. Now peel oranges. Cut peelings into small strips. Chop oranges into small bits. Add these to peaches in stone crock. Lastly, stir in sugar. Cover and allow to stand overnight. In the morning, empty mixture into a large kettle and gradually bring to a boil. Allow to simmer gently for approximately 2 hours while frequently stirring. Mixture will thicken to the consistency of marmalade. Spoon or pour into hot sterilized glasses or jars. Fill each to about ½ inch from top. Set aside to cool. When cold, seal tops with covering of hot melted paraffin wax.

** ** ** ** **

Fisher Ames (1758-1808) worked diligently for the ratification of the *Constitution* in Massachusetts. This dedicated Christian was a Congressman in the First Session of the Congress of the United States when the *Bill of Rights* was developed. He was the man who on August 20, 1789, suggested this wording for the First Amendment: *"Congress shall make no law establishing religion, or to prevent the free exercise thereof, or to infringe the rights of conscience."* Regarding his beliefs as to education, Ames declared: *"Should not the Bible regain the place it once held as a school book? ... the Bible ...should be the principle text in our schools. ..."*

Mrs. Marshall's Strawberry-Gooseberry Jam

4 quarts strawberries   4 quarts gooseberries
8 quarts sugar

Wash strawberries and gooseberries thoroughly in cold water. Drain well. Remove hulls from strawberries and stems from gooseberries and discard. Put all berries in large kettle and stir in sugar. Cover and heat slowly until juice begins to form. Uncover and allow to simmer. Stir frequently, until mixture thickens nicely. Take kettle from fire and spoon into sterilized jars or glasses. Fill each to about ½ inch from top. Set aside to cool. When cold, seal tops with covering of hot melted paraffin wax.

** ** ** ** **

John Marshall (1755-1835) of Virginia served in the Continental Army as a Captain. He was with General Washington at Valley Forge in 1777-78 during the terrible freezing winter. Marshall was later a strong advocate of Virginia ratifying the *Constitution*. President John Adams appointed Marshall to be Chief Justice of the United States Supreme Court in 1801. He held that high post for 34 years. Interestingly enough, it was at Marshall's funeral in 1835 that the Liberty Bell cracked. According to Marshall's daughter: *"He believed in the truth of the Christian Revelation. ... of the supreme divinity of our Saviour ... he thought it his duty to make a public confession of the Saviour."*

10

Early American Pickles, Relishes and Sauces

Special Holiday Dessert Sauce Eaten by the Dickinson Family

¼ cup butter	1 tsp flour
1 egg, beaten	Pinch of salt
1 cup sugar	¼ cup brandy

Put butter, beaten egg, sugar, flour and salt in a cast iron skillet and heat. Blend well until mixture is nice and creamy. Take from stove and add brandy, a little at a time, while continuously beating. Pour over dessert dish while hot.

Note: *Mrs. Dickinson always used this special sauce with berry and other fruit cobblers. She also found it to be excellent with fruit cake and mince pie. And she used it on almost all of her pudding dishes.*

** ** ** ** **

John Dickinson (1732-1808) of Pennsylvania was a member of the Continental Congress and a signer of the *Constitution.* This great Christian patriot met with other delegates less than two months before the signing of the *Declaration of Independence.* He suggested that all members of the Convention subscribe to the following stipulation before being seated: ***"I do profess faith in God the Father, and in Jesus Christ his Eternal Son the true God, and in the Holy Spirit, one God blessed for evermore; and I do acknowledge the Holy Scriptures of the Old and New Testaments to be given by Divine inspiration."***

Crabapple Pickles as Made for Mrs. Pinckney

4 cups vinegar   ½ tsp cloves
8 cups sugar   4 cinnamon sticks
       8 cups crabapples, pared and quartered

Blend together in cooking pot or kettle the vinegar, sugar and cloves. Bring to a boil and drop in the cinnamon sticks. Let cook for 6 minutes while continually stirring. Add quartered crabapples and allow to simmer until tender. Pack in sterilized jars. Fill jars to ¼ inch to top with syrup from kettle and seal. **Note:** *Apples, peaches and pears were pickled by the Pinckney family in exactly the same manner.*

** ** ** ** **

Charles Cotesworth Pinckney (1746-1825) of South Carolina was a Brigadier General during the American Revolution. He studied for a military career at the prestigious Royal Military Academy of France. A wealthy planter in civilian life, this great patriot became General George Washington's Aide-de Camp. Pinckney was a delegate to the Constitutional Convention. He later turned down President Washington's offers of various cabinet positions as well as an appointment on the United States

115

Supreme Court. Pinckney once declared: *"Blasphemy against the Almighty is denying His being ... it is punished ... by fine and imprisonment, for Christianity is part of the laws of the land."*

Sweet Pickle Relish – A Clark Family Favorite

8 quarts green tomatoes
1 cup salt
5 small onions, chopped
1 tsp cinnamon
1 tsp pepper
1 tsp cloves

½ tsp allspice
½ tsp cayenne pepper
5 tsp celery seeds
¾ cup mustard seeds
6 cups sugar
1 quart vinegar

Chop up green tomatoes and put in preserving kettle with the salt. Set aside overnight. Drain off liquid the next morning. Stir in chopped onions with tomatoes in kettle. Add cinnamon, pepper, cloves, allspice celery seeds, mustard seeds, sugar and vinegar. Blend everything thoroughly. Bring to boil and allow mixture to boil for 15 full minutes while constantly stirring. Spoon while hot into sterilized jars and seal.

** ** ** ** **

Abraham Clark (1726-94) seldom remembered with the passage of time, was a staunch Christian patriot and New Jersey signer of the *Declaration of Independence*. Clark had two sons who were captured and tortured by the British. The British offered to release the young men if Clark would refute the American cause. So strong were Abraham Clark's feelings for his country that he courageously refused.

Pickled Onions as Enjoyed by Patrick Henry

8 quarts tiny white onions, peeled
Salt to suit
4 quarts vinegar
8 cups sugar

3 tbls whole cloves
¼ cup stick cinnamon broken
2 tbls horseradish, chopped

2 tsp cayenne pepper

Peel skins off onions and discard. Put onions in stone crock. Cover with brine made by dissolving 4 tablespoons salt for each quart of water used. Cover crock and set aside to stand for 24 hours. Then drain off brine. Pack onions in sterilized jars and set aside. Now combine in a large kettle the vinegar, sugar, cloves, cinnamon, horseradish and cayenne pepper. Bring to boil. Pour this mixture, while hot, over onions packed in jars and seal.

** ** ** ** **

Patrick Henry (1736-99), was young America's greatest orator during the period of the American Revolution. In 1774 he stood and electrified the members of the First Continental Congress held in Philadelphia when he declared: *"The distinctions between Virginians, Pennsylvanians, New Yorkers, and New Englanders are no more. I am not*

118

a Virginian, but an American!" Yes, Patrick Henry stood tall among heroes when America desperately needed unafraid, unselfish men to guide her destiny. And so it is today. This great patriot was Commander-in Chief of the Virginia Militia as well as a Member of the Continental Congress. He once stated: *"It cannot be emphasized too strongly or too often that this great nation was founded not by religionists, but by Christians; not on religions, but on the Gospel of Jesus Christ."* Should we not remember this today?

Mrs. Boudinet's Green Tomato Pickles

10 pounds green tomatoes, washed and sliced	1 quart vinegar
	6 cups water
5 pounds white onions, peeled and sliced	1 cup sugar
	2 tbls celery seed
1 cup salt	2 tbls mustard seed

In a large stone crock, put a layer of sliced green tomatoes and sprinkle with salt. Then put a layer of sliced white onions and sprinkle with salt. Continue this until all tomatoes and onions are used. Cover with a heavy dish to weigh down. Set crock aside and let stand overnight. In the morning, drain well and dump mixture into large kettle. Stir in 2 cups vinegar and 2 cups water. Bring to boil. Drain off liquid. Now add 2 more cups vinegar and 4 more cups water. Stir in sugar, celery seed and mustard seed. Again bring mixture to boil. Allow to slowly simmer for 30 minutes while occasionally stirring so as not to burn. Spoon into sterilized jars and seal.

** ** ** ** **

Elias Boudinot (1740-1821), although a name so often forgotten with the passage of time, was a much respected patriot throughout the Colonies. This great Christian was the Founding Father who in 1783 held the esteemed position as President of the Continental Congress. Nevertheless, most people today would remember this great man as the founder and President of the *American Bible Society*. Boudinot once stated: *"Good government generally begins in the family, and if the moral character of a people once degenerate, their political character must soon follow."*

New England Chow Chow as Prepared for the Chase Family

8 quarts ripe tomatoes, peeled and chopped	1 cup ground mustard
1 quart onions, chopped	1 tbls cinnamon
	1 tbls cloves
1 cup salt	½ tsp cayenne pepper
	1 tbls celery seed
1 pint cider vinegar	

Put peeled and chopped tomatoes in preserving kettle with chopped onions and salt. Set aside for 3 to 4 hours. Then drain off liquid. Bring ingredients in kettle to boil and cook for 2 hours, stirring frequently so as not to burn. Stir in ground mustard, cinnamon, cloves, cayenne pepper, celery seed and cider vinegar. Blend everything thoroughly. Allow to boil for 1 more hour. Spoon into sterilized pint jars and seal.

** ** ** ** **

Samuel Chase (1741-1811), another Christian Founding Father, was appointed to be a Justice of the United States Supreme Court by President George Washington. He was a patriot from Maryland who bravely signed the *Declaration of Independence*. This man once stated: ***"By our form of***

121

government, the Christian religion is the established religion; and all sects and denominations of Christians are placed upon the same equal footing, and are equally entitled to protection in their religious liberty."

The Floyd Family's Best Beet Relish

1 quart beets, cooked and chopped	1 garlic clove, minced
1 head cabbage, chopped	2 cups sugar
1 cup horseradish, grated	2 tbls salt
	2 tsp mustard
	2 tsp celery seed
1 pint vinegar	

Put beets, cabbage, horseradish and garlic in a stone crock and blend thoroughly. Add sugar, salt, mustard, celery seed and vinegar. Stir mixture until everything is nicely blended. Cover crock and let stand at least 24 hours before using. This relish will keep in cool place indefinitely. It may be put in glass jars and sealed or simply left in covered crock until needed.

** ** ** ** **

William Floyd (1734-1821) is not a name to be found in most of today's history books, but this brave New York Christian stood tall against British bondage when he courageously signed the *Declaration of Independence*. In retaliation, the British destroyed his home and laid waste his land. Floyd's wife was forced to flee from Long Island Sound to Connecticut where she passed away in 1781, never again being able to return to their home place. Yes, William Floyd paid dearly for his unwavering stand for liberty and freedom. Yet he never regretted what he had so freely given of himself for the great American cause.

11

Corn Meal Specialties of Yesteryear

The Hampton Family's Apple Corn Bread

2 cups corn meal   3 tsp baking powder
1 tsp baking soda   1 egg, well beaten
3 tbls sugar   2 cups sour milk
2 cups apples, chopped

Sift together the corn meal, baking soda, sugar and baking powder in a wooden mixing bowl. Stir in beaten egg and sour milk. Blend everything thoroughly. Lastly, stir in chopped apple pieces. Pour batter into well greased baking pan. Bake at 400 degrees for 20 to 30 minutes.

** ** ** ** **

Wade Hampton (1754-1835) was a wealthy patriot who fought heroically during the American Revolution. This Christian served his country valiantly as a military leader holding the rank of General in the Continental Army under George Washington's command. He along with many others risked everything fighting for liberty and freedom, yet today they have largely been forgotten with the passage of time.

Brigadier General Greene's Favorite Honey Corn Bread

⅔ cup honey	2 cups flour
½ cup butter, melted	2 tbls baking powder
4 eggs, well beaten	1 tsp salt
2 cups milk	2 cups corn meal

Blend honey and melted butter in a wooden mixing bowl. Stir in beaten eggs and milk. Sift together the flour, baking powder and salt in a separate mixing bowl. Stir the corn meal into this dry mixture. Now add the dry ingredients to honey and butter mixture in first bowl. Stir until everything is nicely blended and moist. Butter two 8-inch square baking pans. Pour batter into pans and bake at 400 degrees for 20 to 25 minutes.

** ** ** ** **

Brigadier General Nathaniel Greene (1742-86) was an officer in George Washington's Continental Army in 1775. He was a Quaker from Rhode Island, but was disowned by his religious sect because of his militaristic leanings. Greene organized three regiments of militia in Rhode Island as an *"Army of Observation"* after the Lexington affair. On June 22, 1775, he was made a Brigadier General as General

George Washington recognized and appreciated his military expertise and leadership qualities. He was soon after promoted to Major General in August of 1776. Greene fought with distinction at Trenton, in Virginia, North Carolina and South Carolina. He returned to Rhode Island after the war was over.

Hominy Corn Bread as Enjoyed by David Kinnison

1 cup hominy, cooked	2 cups white corn meal
2 eggs, well beaten	2 tsp salt
Boiling water as required	2 tbls butter

Put the cold cooked hominy, beaten eggs, white corn meal and salt in a wooden mixing bowl and lightly stir together. Add enough boiling water to make a rather thin batter. Grease two loaf pans, each with 1 tablespoon of the butter, and heat. When loaf pans are hot, pour batter equally into each pan. Bake at 350 degrees for around 40 minutes.

** ** ** ** **

David Kinnison (1736-1851) was a heroic New England patriot who early on took a stand for liberty in the Colonies. This devout Christian was a leader of those Sons of Liberty who demonstrated their disdain for British taxes by dumping a cargo of tea into Boston Harbor in 1773. This defiant act became famous as the "Boston Tea Party." Citizens disguised as Indians took 342 chests from the holds of British ships anchored in Boston Harbor and dumped them into the water. Kinnison's lasting claim to fame is that he was the Boston Tea Party's last survivor when he passed away in 1851.

Johnny Cake as Made by the Aitken Family

1 cup corn meal	1 tsp salt
¼ cup flour	2 eggs
1-½ tsp baking powder	½ cup milk
4 tbls shortening, melted	

Sift together the corn meal, flour, baking powder and salt in a wooden mixing bowl. Beat eggs and milk together in separate bowl. Stir this into dry ingredients in first bowl. Add melted shortening and blend well. Grease a 9 x 9 inch square baking pan. Pour batter into this pan. Bake at 425 degrees for about 25 minutes. When done, cut into 12 squares and serve while hot with butter.

** ** ** ** **

Robert Aitken (1734-1802) was the noted publisher of *The Pennsylvania Magazine.* This great Christian patriot took it upon himself to petition Congress for permission to print *Bibles* in America. The Revolutionary War had so disrupted trade with Great Britain that there was a great shortage of *Bibles* in the former Colonies. Therefore, in response to Aitken's petition, the Continental Congress, on September 10, 1782, agreed that *"a neat edition of the Holy Scriptures for the use of the schools"* be published in Philadelphia. This was the first *Bible* to be published in America and it came about because of Robert Aitken.

Berry Corn Bread – A Peale Family Hand-Me-Down

1 cup berries, dried	1 tbls sugar
1 cup flour	1 tsp salt
¾ cup corn meal	3 tbls butter, melted
2 tsp baking powder	2 eggs, beaten
½ tsp baking soda	1 cup buttermilk

Chop dried berries into small bits. Mix with ¼ cup flour in a wooden mixing bowl. Sift together in the same bowl the remaining ¾ cup flour, corn meal, baking powder, baking soda, sugar and salt. In a separate bowl, blend the melted butter, beaten eggs and buttermilk. Then stir this mixture into the dry ingredients in first bowl. Mix just enough to moisten well. Grease a shallow baking pan. Pour batter into pan and bake at 425 degrees for about 30 minutes. Makes enough to serve 6 people.

** ** ** ** **

Charles Wilson Peale (1741-1827) was a noted American artist-soldier. He was a captain in the Continental Army and saw action at Trenton. Peale was fascinated with military weapons and was known to take time out during battles to make sketches of cannons. He later became famous as a

129

portrait painter. This man, a Christian, was a close friend of George and Martha Washington. He was allowed to paint George's first ever portrait in 1772. Martha at the same time let him paint a beautiful miniature of her.

Mrs. Stockton's Best Corn Bread Receipt

¾ cup corn meal	½ tsp baking soda
1 cup flour	½ tsp salt
¼ cup sugar	1 egg, well beaten
2 tsp baking powder	1 cup sour milk
	3 tbls butter, melted

Sift together in a wooden mixing bowl the corn meal, flour, sugar, baking powder, baking soda and salt. Stir in the well beaten egg, sour milk and melted butter. Beat all ingredients thoroughly. Grease a shallow baking pan. Pour batter into this and bake at 425 degrees for 20 minutes or more.

** ** ** ** **

Richard Stockton (1730-81) was another brave signer of the *Declaration of Independence* and a member of the Continental Congress. He was captured by the British who beat and starved him in an attempt to force him to betray his country and his friends. Stockton was finally freed in a prisoner exchange but was by then an invalid. As a result of British brutality, this unsung American hero died at the early age of 51. Stockton was a true patriot who believed in the cause of freedom so fervently that he willingly and unselfishly sacrificed everything in order to see it come to pass. Regarding his faith, he declared: ***"I think it proper here, not only to subscribe to the entire belief ... of the Christian religion ... remember, 'that the fear of the Lord is the beginning of wisdom."***

The Wilson Family's Special Corn Bread Receipt

1 cup milk	1-½ cups corn meal
1 cup molasses	1 tbls ginger
1 tbls butter, well rounded	2 eggs, well beaten

Combine milk and molasses in saucepan and heat. When hot, dissolve butter in this mixture. Add corn meal, ginger and beaten eggs. Beat together thoroughly. Grease a cast iron skillet. Pour batter into skillet. Bake at 350 degrees for 30 to 40 minutes or until browned on top.

** ** ** ** **

James Wilson (1742-98) was a man of Scottish birth who came to America and became a patriot in the cause of freedom and liberty. He was appointed by President George Washington as an Associate Justice of the United States Supreme Court in 1789. Prior to this, Wilson holds the distinction of being only one of six Founding Fathers to have signed both the *Declaration of Independence* and the *Constitution.* This devout Christian was an extremely active participant in the Constitutional Convention. He is known to have spoken 168 times. Always busy, Wilson also became the University of Pennsylvania's first Law Professor.

12

Bread and Rolls as Made by Homemakers in the Colonies

Bread Receipt of the Oglethorpe Family

1 package dry yeast	5 cups flour
2 cups water, lukewarm	2 tsp salt

Sprinkle dry yeast in a wooden mixing bowl with the lukewarm water. Let it dissolve thoroughly. Then stir in flour and salt and blend until soft dough is formed. Knead 5 times. Place dough in well-greased bowl. Butter the top of dough. Cover with towel and set aside in warm place to rise – about 1 hour. Then divide dough into 7 equal sized balls. Dip hands in flour to keep dough from sticking. Cover dough balls with towel and set aside to rise for 15 minutes. Roll out each dough ball into an 8 inch circle. They will look like thick pancakes. Again cover with towel and let rise for 45 minutes more. Place empty cookie sheets in oven and preheat to 500 degrees. Then turn oven to *broil*. Place dough on hot cookie sheets and broil on both sides until light brown. Watch carefully so as not to burn. Remove from oven and wrap in cloth.

** ** ** ** **

133

James Edward Oglethorpe (1696-1785) was a well known British General. This man was granted a charter in 1732 by King George II. He came over to the Colonies with a large entourage of poor immigrants in 1733. As these settlers first disembarked from the ship, they kneeled and prayed: *"Our end in leaving our native country is not to gain riches and honor, but singly this: to live wholly to the glory of God."* Oglethorpe's purpose was to found the Crown Colony of Georgia. This he did in 1752. He is credited with founding the city of Savannah. Strong drink and slavery were prohibited. The first settlers were required to plant mulberry trees for silk worms, with the idea that the colony would produce silk. This didn't work out for a number of reasons. Today, James Edward Oglethorpe is best remembered as "The Father of Georgia."

Rufus King's Famous Molasses Gingerbread

2 cups flour	¼ tsp cinnamon
2 tsp baking powder	¼ tsp cloves
½ tsp salt	2 eggs, well beaten
¼ tsp baking soda	¾ cup molasses
½ cup sugar	½ cup sour milk
½ tsp ginger	½ cup butter, melted

Sift together in a large wooden mixing bowl the flour, baking powder, salt, baking soda, sugar, ginger, cinnamon and cloves. In a separate bowl, blend the beaten eggs, molasses, sour milk and melted butter. Add this mixture to the dry ingredients in first bowl and blend everything thoroughly to a smooth batter. Pour batter into greased 8-inch cake pans or into muffin tins. Bake cake pans at 375 degrees for 30 to 35 minutes. Bake muffin tins for 20 to 25 minutes.

** ** ** ** **

Rufus King (1755-1827) was a noted Christian statesman and member of the Federalist Party, but pretty much a forgotten man with the passage of time. King, along with Elbridge Gerry, both from Massachusetts, had a great deal to do with the work on the *Constitution* at the Constitutional

Convention in 1787. This brilliant thinker was one of the Convention's youngest delegates at only 32 years old. He strongly objected to setting a date for Congress to meet each year. King felt it wasn't necessary and perhaps dangerous. His exact words were: *"A great vice in our system was that of legislating too much."* King's words may have turned out to have been prophetic.

David Brearly's Favorite Pocketbook Rolls

1 cup water, boiling	½ yeast cake
2 tbls butter	½ cup water, lukewarm
1 tsp salt	3-½ cups flour
¼ cup sugar	1 egg, well beaten

Put boiling water in large wooden mixing bowl. Stir in butter, salt and sugar. Blend thoroughly. Meanwhile, crumble yeast cake in lukewarm water and let it dissolve completely. When dissolved, stir this into mixture in bowl. Sift flour into bowl and blend with other ingredients. When done, cover and set aside in warm place to rise. When double in bulk, add well beaten egg. Knead lightly. Roll out to ½ inch thick on well-floured board. Cut with upside down glass about 3 inches in diameter. Crease each roll in center with dull knife. Brush with melted butter. Fold over. Pinch dough at sides to make pocketbook. Brush tops with melted butter. Set aside to rise. Place on greased cookie sheet. Bake at 390 degrees for about 20 minutes.

** ** ** ** **

David Brearly (1745-1790) is an often forgotten Christian patriot who had much to do in the formulation of our great nation's beginnings. He fought courageously under General Washington as a Colonel in the Continental Army during the War for American Independence. Later on, he was a signer of our *Constitution*. Brearly was another of the Founding Fathers who attended Princeton and studied under the most influential Reverend John Witherspoon. He was once arrested by the British for "high treason" because of his fearless outspokenness regarding the cause of liberty. Brearly, according to Tim LaHaye, was, among many other things, "*a compiler of the **Protestant Episcopal Prayer Book**.*"

The Nelson Family's Method of Making Good White Bread

1 yeast cake	2 tbls butter, melted
2 tbls sugar	12 cups flour
4 cups water, lukewarm	1 tbls salt

Crumble yeast cake in wooden mixing bowl. Add sugar and lukewarm water. Stir until yeast is completely dissolved. Add melted butter and 6 cups flour. Beat mixture until smooth. Add salt and rest of the flour, or just enough flour to make dough that can be handled nicely. Knead dough until smooth and elastic. Place dough in greased bowl. Cover and set aside in moderately warm place, free from drafts, until light – about 2 hours. Then mold into loaves. Place in well-greased bread pans. Fill each pan about ½ full. Cover with towel. Set aside and let rise 1 hour or until double in bulk. Bake at 350 degrees for 40 to 50 minutes.

** ** ** ** **

Thomas Nelson (1738-85) was another heroic signer of the *Declaration of Independence*. He was also the fearless Commander of the 3,000 member Virginia Militia. Nelson, a devout Christian, declared: *"I call to God to witness that if any British troops are landed in the county of York ... I will wait no orders, but will summon the militia and drive the invaders into the sea."* This courageous and dedicated man actually ordered the destruction of his own mansion when it was being used as a headquarters for the British. Nelson died in poverty as a result of his signing the *Declaration* and the War for American Independence.

Mrs. Paterson's German Unfermented Bread

4 cups flour	2 cups water
3 tbls sugar	2 tsp baking powder
1 tbls lard, melted	1 egg
	1 tbls salt

Blend together in a large wooden mixing bowl the flour, sugar, melted lard, water, baking powder, egg and salt. Work well until a smooth dough is formed. Mold into the shape of a loaf. Don't handle much, but immediately place dough in greased square baking pan. Put in oven and bake at 350 degrees for about 1 hour. Test with a toothpick for doneness.

** ** ** ** **

William Paterson (1745-1806) was another great American patriot with whom the passage of time has not been kind. He contributions in our nation's history have often been forgotten. This devout Christian attended Princeton and of the 18 members of his class, 12 became ministers. He was a member of the Continental Congress from New Jersey and a signer of our *Constitution*. President George Washington appointed him to be an Associate Justice of the United States Supreme Court in 1793. So esteemed was this man in the eyes of the people of his state that they named the city of Paterson after him.

The Hamilton Family's Blood Bread Receipt

1 yeast cake
1-⅓ cups water, lukewarm
10 cups flour
1-⅓ cups uncoagulated beef blood

Crumble yeast cake in large wooden mixing bowl and mix with lukewarm water. When completely dissolved, add enough flour to make a thin batter. Put balance of flour in large pan and make a hollow in center. Pour batter from mixing bowl in the hollow and sprinkle a little flour over the top. Cover pan with a towel. Put in warm place for ½ hour to rise. When ferment has risen (when the flour sprinkled on top begins to crack) add 1-⅓ cups lukewarm water in which 1/8 cup salt has been dissolved. Then add beef blood. Work into a smooth, soft dough. Knead thoroughly and mold into loaves. Bake at 350 degrees for 40 to 50 minutes or until done. Test for doneness with a toothpick. Makes four nice 1 pound loaves.

** ** ** ** **

Alexander Hamilton (1757-1804) was born in the West Indies and didn't come to the Colonies until 1772. Yet he joined in the fight for American independence and became one of the Republic's brightest stars. Hamilton was one of George Washington's closest friends and most trusted advisors during the War for Independence. He later became President Washington's Secretary of the Treasury. A brilliant essayist, his writings urged the ratification of the *Constitution*. These essays were later published as *The Federalist* with contributions from John Jay and James Madison as well. Hamilton's life was ended when he was mortally wounded in a duel with Aaron Burr, former Vice-President under Thomas Jefferson. His dying words were: *"I have a tender reliance on the mercy of the Almighty, through the merits of the Lord Jesus Christ. I am a sinner. I look to Him for mercy; pray for me."*

13

Biscuits and Muffins – An Old-Fashioned Delight

Apple Muffins – a Specialty of the Read Family

1 egg, well beaten	2-½ tsp baking powder
1 cup milk	½ tsp salt
⅓ cup shortening, melted	4 tbls sugar
2 cups flour	½ tsp cinnamon

¾ cup apple, grated

Put beaten egg, milk and melted shortening in wooden mixing bowl. Beat until thoroughly blended. Sift together in a separate bowl the flour, baking powder, salt, sugar and cinnamon. Add dry ingredients to those in first bowl. Stir only until everything is nicely moistened. Lastly, add grated apple and blend well. Pour batter into well-greased muffin pans. Bake at 400 degrees for 25 minutes.

** ** ** ** **

George Read (1733-98) was a delegate from Delaware to the Constitutional Convention. A true American patriot, this man holds the distinction of being a signer of both the *Declaration of Independence* and the *Constitution*. A devout Christian, Read studied at the seminary in New London under Reverend Allison. His father-in law was the pastor for 50 years of the Immanuel Church in Newcastle.

The McKean Family's Cheese Biscuits

2 cups flour

2-½ tsp baking powder

½ tsp salt

¼ cup shortening

½ cup cheddar cheese, grated

¾ cup milk

Sift together in wooden mixing bowl the flour, salt and baking powder. Cut shortening into dry ingredients with fork until mixture looks like coarse corn meal. Blend in grated cheddar cheese. Punch a concave well in center of mixture. Add milk and stir quickly until thoroughly blended. Mixture should be soft but not sticky. Turn onto lightly floured board. Knead lightly about 10 to 15 strokes. Pat or roll out to ¼ inch thick for thin crusty biscuits or ½ inch thick for soft biscuits. Cut with lightly floured biscuit cutter or overturned water glass. Place on ungreased baking sheet. Bake at 450 degrees for 12 to 15 minutes or until golden brown. Makes about 16 biscuits.

** ** ** ** **

Thomas McKean (1734-1817) was a great American patriot who most Americans have forgotten with the passage of time. This man stood for freedom when he bravely signed the *Declaration of Independence*. He ended up paying dearly for his efforts. McKean, a Christian, was hounded by the British in an effort to force him to renounce his signing of the *Declaration*. He had to constantly keep his family in hiding. He later served in Congress without pay. Everything this great man owned was confiscated by the British and he died in rags. But Thomas McKean never lost his faith in God and the rightness of what he had done for his country and his fellow citizens.

Bacon Muffins – As Enjoyed by John Paul Jones

2 cups flour   ½ cup fried bacon,
3 tbls sugar   crisp and chopped
2-½ tsp baking powder   1 egg, well beaten
½ tsp salt   1 cup milk
                    3 tbls bacon grease

Sift together in a wooden mixing bowl the flour, sugar, baking powder and salt. Stir in the crispy chopped bacon pieces. In a separate wooden bowl, combine beaten egg, milk and cooled melted bacon grease. Make a well in dry ingredients. Pour in the liquid mixture. Stir just enough to lightly blend. The mixture should have a rather rough appearance. Grease muffin pan and fill ⅔ full. Bake at 400 to 425 degrees for about 20 to 30 minutes. Makes approximately 12 muffins.

** ** ** ** **

John Paul Jones (1747-92) was born in Scotland under the name of John Paul. He engaged in the slave trade from 1766 and some years afterwards, later relocating in Virginia where he took on the name John Paul Jones. Congress commissioned him as a naval officer in 1775 and he was quickly given command of a naval vessel. Jones became a notable figure during the Revolutionary War because of his daring exploits. He is sometimes acclaimed to be the *"Father of the American Navy"* because of his inspirational and heroic deeds at sea. After all this great Christian patriot did for the American cause, when the war was over, he left and served for a time in the Russian navy. He then died, sadly enough, in obscurity.

James Madison's Favorite Baking Powder Biscuits

2 cups flour	½ tsp salt
2-½ tsp baking powder	¼ cup butter, melted
¾ cup milk (about)	

Sift together in a wooden mixing bowl the flour, baking powder and salt. Pour the cooled melted butter into this dry mixture. Stir until mixture becomes grainy and resembles coarse corn meal. Make a well in center and add milk. Stir lightly until nicely blended. Mixture should be soft but not sticky. Dump out onto lightly floured board. Knead about 10 to 15 strokes. Pat or roll out to ¼ inch for thin crusty biscuits or ½ inch thick for soft biscuits. Cut with floured biscuit cutter or overturned water glass. Place on ungreased baking sheet. Bake at 450 degrees for 12 to 15 minutes or until golden brown. Makes about 16 biscuits.

** ** ** ** **

James Madison (1751-1836) was the 4th President of the United States who served his country in this position from 1809 to 1817. He was one of the most influential leaders at the Constitutional Convention and favored a strong central government. This great patriot collaborated with John Jay and Alexander Hamilton in writing *The Federalist Papers*. He served in the Continental Congress, was Secretary of State under Thomas Jefferson, and is known today as the *"Father of the Constitution."* Madison strongly supported the *Bill of Rights* and was the man who pushed it through Congress. James Madison outlived all of the other 54 Founders of our Republic. He once said this: *"We have all been encouraged to feel in the guardianship and guidance of that Almighty Being, whose power regulates the destiny of nations."*

Molly Pitcher's Cranberry Muffins

½ cup butter	¼ cup baking powder
⅔ cup sugar	1-½ tsp salt
4 eggs, beaten	1-⅓ cups milk
4 cups flour	1-½ cups cranberries

Cream butter and sugar in wooden mixing bowl. Add beaten eggs and blend well. Sift together in a separate bowl the flour, baking powder and salt. Add this to the first mixture. Lastly add milk and cranberries. Blend everything thoroughly. Grease muffin tins and fill ⅔ full. Bake at 400 degrees for 30 minutes.

** ** ** ** **

Molly McKolly was a young, *Bible* believing Christian heroine during the Revolutionary War. She accompanied her husband onto the battlefield during the Battle of Monmouth on June 28, 1778. Molly carried water in a pitcher to her husband and other soldiers, thereby earning her the nickname, "Molly Pitcher." When her husband was wounded and collapsed in the 100 degree heat, Molly quickly took his place and kept right on firing his cannon. In his war memoir, Joseph Plumb Martin of Connecticut, a soldier who saw this woman under fire, wrote: ***"While in the act of reaching for a cartridge, a cannon shot from the enemy passed directly between her legs ... carrying away the lower part of her petticoat."*** The Pennsylvania legislature finally passed a special act in 1822 that read: ***"For the relief of Molly McKolly for her services during the Revolutionary War."*** She was given $40.00 and was to be paid $40.00 a year for the rest of her life. Molly died on May 22, 1832. And a monument honoring this heroic woman today sits beside her gravesite in Carlisle, Pennsylvania.

Ham Biscuits – A Favorite of the Hewes Family

2 cups flour	⅔ cup milk
2 tsp baking powder	2 tbls butter, melted
½ tsp salt	½ cup ham, minced
4 tbls ham grease	2 tsp mustard

Sift flour and measure out 2 cups. Then sift together in a wooden mixing bowl the flour, baking powder and salt. Stir in ham grease. Gradually add milk. Work in with hands until soft dough is formed. Turn dough out onto lightly floured board and knead a little – no more than 15 strokes. Pat or roll dough out into 1/8 inch thick sheet. Cut with floured biscuit cutter or upside down water glass. Lay half the biscuits on well greased baking sheet. Brush with melted butter. Now mix minced ham and mustard in small bowl or cup. Put equal amount of this mixture on top of each biscuit on baking sheet. Lay other biscuits on top of these. Press down lightly. Brush top of each biscuit with a little milk. Bake at 450 degrees for about 12 minutes. Serve while piping hot. Makes approximately 12 servings.

** ** ** ** **

Joseph Hewes (1730-79) of North Carolina, signer of the *Declaration of Independence*, was a Quaker and a pacifist. After much soul searching, this brave Christian patriot declared: ***"My country is entitled to my services, and I shall not shrink from the cause, even though it should cost me my life."*** He died in 1779, shunned by his Quaker family and friends, none who could understand or accept what he had done.

The Muhlenberg Family's Maple Sugar Muffins

2 cups flour	½ cup nuts, chopped
4 tbls maple sugar	1 egg, well beaten
2-½ tsp baking powder	1 cup milk
½ tsp salt	4 tbls butter, melted

Sift together in a wooden mixing bowl the flour, maple sugar, baking powder and salt. Stir in chopped nuts. In a separate bowl combine beaten egg, milk and cooled melted butter. Make a well in dry ingredients. Pour liquid mixture into this. Stir just enough to lightly blend. The mixture should have a rough appearance. Grease a muffin pan and fill ⅔ full. Bake at 400 to 425 degrees for 20 to 30 minutes or until golden brown.

** ** ** ** **

John Peter Gabriel Muhlenberg (1746-1807) was a patriot and a well known Lutheran pastor like his father, Henry. In 1775, he was preaching to his congregation from Ecclesiastes 3:1 – *"For everything there is a season, and a time for every matter under heaven."* He ended his sermon by declaring: *"In the language of the Holy Writ, there is a time for all things. There is a time to preach and a time to fight!"* He then threw open his robe to reveal his uniform – that of a soldier in the Continental Army. Later that same day, with 300 men under his command, he marched off to join General Washington's troops. Muhlenberg fought throughout the Revolutionary War and was subsequently promoted to the rank of Major General.

14

Cakes of the Past to be Fondly Remembered

Special Pound Cake as Made by the Heyward Family

1 pound butter	3 tbls brandy
1 pound sugar	1 pound flour
10 egg yolks, beaten until thick	½ tsp mace
10 egg whites, beaten stiff	

Using a fork, cream the butter in a wooden mixing bowl. Gradually beat in sugar until all of it is used up. Add thickly beaten egg yolks to butter-sugar mixture. Then blend in the brandy. In a separate bowl, sift together the flour and mace. Add this alternately, with the stiffly beaten egg whites, to mixture in the first bowl. Pour into nicely buttered loaf pan. Bake at 300 degrees for 1-1/2 hours.

** ** ** ** **

Thomas Heyward Jr. (1746-1809) of South Carolina was another heroic Christian signer of the *Declaration of Independence*. Heyward was captured by the British in the battle defending Charleston. He was offered amnesty if he would repudiate the American cause. Heyward defiantly refused his British captors at the risk of his life. His wife died while he was imprisoned in the Crown Stockade at St. Augustine, Florida.

Apple Coffee Cake from the Benjamin Lincoln Family

1 cup apples, dried and finely chopped

1 cup honey	1 tsp baking soda
1 cup sugar	1 tsp cloves
1 cup soft butter	1 tsp cinnamon
2 eggs	1 tsp allspice
½ cup strong coffee	Flour as required

Put dried apples in saucepan with a little water. Bring to boil and allow to stew for 10 minutes or until soft. Then add honey, and allow to simmer another hour. Set aside to cool. Meanwhile, in a large wooden mixing bowl, cream together the sugar and butter. Then beat in eggs, coffee, baking soda, cloves, cinnamon and allspice. When mixture in saucepan has cooled, stir it into ingredients in mixing bowl. Lastly, work in enough flour to make stiff batter. Butter and flour shallow baking pan. Pour batter into this. Bake at 375 degrees until done.

** ** ** ** **

General Benjamin Lincoln (1733-1810) was a great Christian leader during the American War for Independence. Lincoln fought in numerous campaigns throughout the war. When the British finally surrendered at Yorktown, Cornwallis, in an attempt to embarrass what he considered to be the Colonial upstarts, would not personally appear to go through the formality of handing over his sword. He lied when he sent word to General Washington that he was ill. His second in command, General Charles O'Hara led the British troops to the surrender point in his place. O'Hara tried to hand his sword to General Rochambeau who refused to accept it. Next General Washington refused it. O'Hara was then passed on to General Lincoln who was allowed to accept.

Honey Cake as Enjoyed by John Adams

½ cup butter
1 cup honey
1 egg, well beaten
2 cups flour, sifted

1 tsp baking soda
½ tsp salt
½ tsp cinnamon
½ cup sour milk

Using a fork, cream butter in wooden mixing bowl. Stir in honey and beaten egg. Sift together in separate bowl the flour, baking soda, salt and cinnamon. Add this alternately with sour milk, to mixture in first bowl. Blend everything thoroughly. Butter a shallow baking pan. Pour mixture into this. Bake at 350 degrees for 50 minutes. When done, take from pan and set aside to cool. Meanwhile, make the following frosting:

1 cup powdered sugar
1-1/2 tbls milk, warm

1 tbls butter. melted
½ tsp honey, warm

Blend powdered sugar, warm milk, melted butter and warm honey in a wooden mixing bowl. Spread over entire cake when it has completely cooled.

** ** ** ** **

John Adams (1735-1826) was a patriot and Revolutionary leader with his cousin Samuel Adams for more than 20 years prior to the American Revolution. He was a member of the Continental Congress and a signer of the *Declaration of Independence.* As Minister to France, he along with Benjamin Franklin and John Jay assisted in the negotiations for a treaty with England to end the Revolutionary War. He was a major force behind getting the various American states to ratify the *Constitution.* Was John Adams a Christian? Here's what he told Thomas Jefferson in a letter dated November 4, 1816: ***"The Ten Commandments and the Sermon on the Mount contain my religion. ..."*** In a previous correspondence with Jefferson, he wrote: ***"I have examined all religions ... and the result is that the Bible is the best Book in the world."***

Early American Cruller Receipt from the Middleton Family

¼ cup butter   4 cups flour
1 cup sugar   ¼ tsp nutmeg, grated
2 egg yolks, beaten   3-½ tsp baking powder
2 egg whites, beaten stiff   1 cup milk
              Powdered sugar as required
              Cinnamon as required

Cream butter and sugar together in a wooden mixing bowl. Then stir in beaten egg yolks. Fold in stiffly beaten egg whites. Blend together in a separate bowl the flour, grated nutmeg and baking powder. Add this, alternately, with the milk to mixture in first bowl. Blend everything thoroughly. Dump onto floured board. Roll out to a ¼ inch thick sheet. Cut into 8 inch long by ½ inch wide strips. Twist strips together or braid 3 strips together. Press ends together flat. Lower into hot grease and fry until nicely browned. Drain well on absorbent paper. Lastly, roll each cruller in powdered sugar and cinnamon.

** ** ** ** **

Arthur Middleton (1742-87) from South Carolina was another great American patriot who bravely signed the *Declaration of Independence*. Middleton was captured by the British in Charleston and was offered his freedom if only he would agree to repudiate the American cause. He adamantly refused! Middleton was subsequently imprisoned in the Crown Stockade at St. Augustine, Florida, where the British subjected him to severe beatings and many indignities. He was finally released in a prisoner exchange in 1781.

Fruit Cake as Made for George Washington

2 cups butter	4 cups flour
3 cups sugar	3 tsp baking powder
5 egg whites, beaten	½ tsp cinnamon
5 egg yolks, beaten	¼ tsp nutmeg
1 cup milk	2 cups raisins, floured

Handful citron, chopped and floured
2 cups hickory nuts, chopped

Cream butter and sugar in large wooden mixing bowl. Lightly stir in beaten egg whites. Then stir in beaten egg yolks. Add milk and blend mixture well. In a separate bowl, sift together the flour, baking powder, cinnamon and nutmeg. Stir this into mixture in first bowl. After all ingredients are blended, stir in chopped citron and chopped hickory nuts. Line loaf pans with well-buttered paper. Pour batter into pans. Bake at 275 degrees for at least 2 hours. **Note:** *Martha Washington was given this special recipe by her mother on her wedding day. It was said to be often used during the Christmas holidays by the family.*

** ** ** ** **

George Washington (1732-99), a man who was formally taught school only to the elementary level, went on to become Commander-in Chief of the Continental Army in 1775. This great and revered American also served his country as Chairman of the Constitutional Convention. He went on to further serve his country as its first President from 1789 to 1797. Washington, *"Without making ostentatious professions of religion, was a sincere believer in the Christian faith, and a truly devout man,"* according to John Marshall, Chief Justice of the United States Supreme Court. Marshall, a close friend of Washington, had fought beside him at Valley Forge during the Revolutionary War. When first leaving home to serve his country, Washington wrote down the parting words of his mother, Mrs. Mary Washington: *"Remember that God is our only sure trust. To Him, I commend you. ...My son, neglect not the duty of secret prayer."*

Maple Crumble Coffee Cake Breakfast Squares – A Samuel West Favorite

1 yeast cake	1 tsp salt
¼ cup water, lukewarm	¼ cup butter, soft
1 cup milk, scalded	3-¼ cups flour, sifted
¼ cup maple sugar	1 egg

Crumble yeast cake in the lukewarm water and stir until completely dissolved. Meanwhile put scalded milk in a wooden mixing bowl and stir in maple sugar, salt and soft butter. Allow to cool until it is lukewarm. Then add 2 cups of the flour. Beat thoroughly with a spoon until well blended. Add yeast and egg. Beat well again with spoon. Add remaining flour to make a thick batter. Beat until smooth and free of lumps. Cover with towel and set in warm place to rise until doubled in size. Stir down. Lightly butter two 8 x 8 x 2 inch baking pans. Pour batter evenly into these pans. Set aside and prepare the following topping:

½ cup flour	1 tsp cinnamon
½ cup bread crumbs	4 tbls butter
4 tbls maple sugar	½ cup nuts, chopped

Combine flour, bread crumbs, maple sugar and cinnamon in a wooden mixing bowl. Cut in butter with a fork until mixture is crumbly. Lastly add the chopped nuts and blend well. Spread evenly over batter in each baking pan with floured finger tips. Divide into nine squares by taking knife and pressing lines deep into batter. Again cover and set aside in warm place to rise for 50 minutes. Then bake at 350 degrees for 20 to 25 minutes.

** ** ** ** **

Samuel West (1731-1807) hold the unique distinction of being the official Chaplain for the Continental Army during the Revolutionary War. This outstanding Christian patriot was able to greatly help General Washington when he exposed a treasonous letter written by Dr. Benjamin Church to the British Admiral in Newport, Rhode Island. West was also a member of the Massachusetts Convention, which adopted the *United States Constitution.*

Mrs. Lee's Special Maple Syrup Cake

½ cup butter	2 tsp baking powder
½ cup sugar	½ tsp baking soda
1 cup maple syrup	⅔ tsp ginger
2 eggs, beaten	½ cup water, boiling
2-½ cups flour	1 cup nuts, chopped

Cream butter and sugar together in a wooden mixing bowl. Stir in maple syrup and blend thoroughly. Add beaten eggs and stir well. Sift together in a separate bowl the flour, baking powder, baking soda and ginger. Add this, a little at a time, alternately, with the boiling water, to mixture in first bowl. Beat thoroughly after each addition. Lastly, stir in the chopped nuts. Butter a loaf pan. Pour batter into this. Bake at 350 degrees for 45 minutes. When done, take from loaf pan and allow to cool. Meanwhile, make the following special frosting:

2 cups maple sugar	1 cup cream
⅛ tsp salt	¾ cup nuts, chopped fine

Blend maple sugar, salt and cream in small kettle. Bring mixture to a boil. Let simmer until a little dropped into cold water forms a soft ball. Then pour out into a bowl. Stir in

the chopped nuts.   Beat until creamy.   Allow to cool.
Carefully spread over cake.

** ** ** ** **

   Richard Henry Lee (1732-1794), a Virginian, was a
direct descendant of some of the earliest settlers in the
Colonies. This great American patriot was a man of strong
Christian convictions. He became one of the early heroes in
the Colonies when he openly came out in favor of
independence in defiance of British rule. Lee was a delegate
to both the First and Second Continental Congress. He was
the man who bravely introduced the resolution for
independence before the Continental Congress on July 2,
1776.   And Richard Henry Lee was also the man who
proposed the *10th Amendment* to the *Constitution*, which
specifically limited the power of the Federal Government.

15

Cookies as Made in the Kitchens of Long, Long Ago

The Quincy Family's Molasses Snaps

1 cup sugar   1 cup molasses
1 cup butter

Put sugar, molasses and butter in a small cast iron kettle and let come to a boil. Immediately take from the fire and set aside to cool slightly. Then add the following ingredients:

5 cups flour   1 tps salt
¾ tsp baking powder

Blend everything thoroughly. Dump dough out onto a lightly floured board. Roll out to about a 1/8 inch thick sheet. Cut into 2 to 3 inch rounds with a floured cookie cutter or an upside down drinking glass. Put cookies on lightly greased baking sheets. Bake at 400 degrees for about 12 minutes.

** ** ** ** **

Josiah Quincy (1744-75) was another American patriot who is often forgotten with the passage of time but this man was a firebrand during the Colonial period of our history. So respected was he as an orator and untiring supporter of the Revolution that he was sent on a special mission to England in 1774 to argue the cause of the Colonies. Sadly enough, this great patriot died while at sea. When the British blockaded Boston Harbor in 1774, Quincy declared: *"... under God, we are determined that wheresoever, or howsoever, we shall be called to make our exit, we will die free men."*

Ben Franklin's Favorite Honey Cookies

⅔ cup butter
½ cup sugar
1 cup honey
1 egg, beaten
½ cup sour cream
½ tsp salt

5 cups flour
1 tsp baking soda
½ tsp cinnamon
½ tsp nutmeg
½ tsp cloves

Using a fork, cream butter and sugar together in a wooden mixing bowl. Add honey and blend thoroughly. Stir in beaten egg along with sour cream. In a separate bowl, sift together the flour, baking soda, cinnamon, nutmeg, cloves and salt. Combine this mixture with ingredients in first bowl and set aside to chill. When cold, dump onto floured board. Roll out to about ¼ inch thick. Cut into 2 to 3 inch rounds with a floured cookie cutter or upside down drinking glass. Lightly grease baking sheets. Place cookie rounds on sheets. Bake at 350 degrees for 10 to 12 minutes. Makes about 4 dozen cookies.

** ** ** ** **

Benjamin Franklin (1706-90), the oldest signer of the *Declaration of Independence*, also signed the *Constitution*. He was the 15th of 17 children in his family and was considered to be a literary genius. Founder of the University of Pennsylvania, Franklin as an inventor made numerous important discoveries and became known as "The Newton of his Age." He organized the first postal system, first volunteer fire department, and street lighting. On Thursday, June 28, 1787, Franklin delivered a powerful speech at the Constitutional Convention. In it he made this long remembered declaration: *"I have lived, Sir, a long time, and the longer I live, the more convincing proofs I see of this truth – that God Governs in the affairs of men. And if a sparrow cannot fall to the ground without His notice, is it probable that an empire can rise without His aid?"*

Wine Drop Cookies as Made by the Williamson Family

⅔ cup butter	¼ tsp cloves
½ cup sugar	½ tsp salt
1 cup light molasses	2 tsp baking soda
1 tsp cinnamon	1 cup water, boiling
1 tsp ginger	4 cups flour

1 cup raisins, cut up

Using a fork, cream butter and sugar together in a wooden mixing bowl. Then stir in molasses, cinnamon, ginger, cloves and salt. Dissolve baking soda in the cup of boiling water. Stir this into mixture in bowl. Fold flour in slowly, blending well, so as not to have lumps in batter. Lastly work in raisins. Lightly grease some cookie sheets. Drop batter by tablespoonfuls onto sheets. Sprinkle with sugar. Bake at 350 degrees for 12 to 15 minutes. Makes about 4 dozen cookies.

** ** ** ** **

Hugh Williamson (1735-1819) is another long forgotten patriot who had much to do as a Founding Father of this great country. He was a member of the Continental Congress and a signer of the *Constitution*. Few people today realize that this man was a brilliant scientist and inventor who often worked with Benjamin Franklin on many of his electrical experiments. Williamson was a devout Christian who as a young man studied for the ministry. Much of his youth was devoted to visiting the sick and praying with them. He later went on to become a minister.

The Rutledge Family's Ginger Cream Cookies

4-½ cups flour	1 cup butter
3 tsp ginger	1 cup sugar
1 tsp baking soda	2 eggs, well beaten
1 tsp salt	½ cup dark molasses

Sift together in a wooden mixing bowl the flour, ginger, baking soda and salt. In a separate bowl, using a fork, cream together the butter and sugar. Add beaten eggs, molasses and 1 cup of the flour mix from first bowl to this. Beat thoroughly until smooth. Then add the remaining dry ingredients and blend well. Put dough on lightly floured board. Make into 2 inch diameter rolls. Wrap rolls in wax paper. Set aside to chill. When rolls of dough are firm, slice about 1 inch thick. Lay each slice on lightly buttered cookie sheets. Bake at 350 degrees for 10 to 12 minutes. Makes about 6 dozen cookies.

** ** ** ** **

Edward Rutledge (1749-1800) of South Carolina, a man with strong Christian convictions, was the youngest signer of the *Declaration of Independence* at 26, while Benjamin Franklin was the oldest at 70 years. John Adams scathingly characterized the delegates with his busy pen. Regarding Rutledge, he noted that Edward was an *"uncouth and ungraceful speaker ... and speaks through his nose ..."* Nevertheless, all of the signers were courageous, public minded citizens who were naturally well off – respected doctors, educators, clergymen, wealthy farmers, prosperous merchants, etc. They all had everything to lose for their act of defiance to the British Crown. But everyone of them were willing to gamble for liberty and freedom and independence for all who were to follow in the years to come.

Thomas Jefferson Style Macaroons

1 pound almonds   ¾ pound powdered sugar
3 eggs, whites only

Put almonds in small kettle and pour boiling water over them. Stir well and remove skins. Wash thoroughly with cold water. Dry well with clean towel. Put in food chopper and grind to fine consistency. Now put in a wooden mixing bowl and gradually beat in the powdered sugar with wooden mixing spoon. Lastly beat in the egg whites, one at a time, until smooth paste is obtained. Using a teaspoon, drop in small nut-size balls on white paper. Bake at 275 degrees for 15 to 20 minutes. Set aside to cool.

** ** ** ** **

Thomas Jefferson (1743-1826) of Virginia was the author of the *Declaration of Independence*. He was young America's third President from 1801 to 1809 following George Washington and John Adams. An innovative individual, Jefferson was the first President to have meringue put on pies served at White House functions. This great man founded the University of Virginia and actually designed the early buildings for the school. He served in the Continental Congress. Jefferson died exactly 50 years after the signing of the *Declaration of Independence*, on July 4th, 1826. Many today make the absurd claim that this patriot was not a Christian, but let Thomas Jefferson speak for himself in this regard. He said quite clearly: ***"There is only one God, and He is perfect. ... Had the doctrines of Jesus been preached always as pure as they came from his lips, the whole civilized world would now have been Christians."***

Almond Roll Ups – A Samuel Adams Family Favorite

¾ cup butter   2 cups flour
1 cup sugar   ¼ tsp salt
1 egg   ½ tsp baking powder
1 tsp vanilla
1 cup almonds, blanched and chopped

Using a fork, cream butter and sugar together in wooden mixing bowl. Then beat in egg and vanilla. In a separate bowl, sift together the flour, salt and baking powder. Add finely chopped almonds to this and stir well. Put dry mixture in first bowl with other ingredients and blend thoroughly. Dump out onto floured board. Form dough into long roll about 2 inches in diameter. Wrap in oiled paper. Set aside on ice to chill for about 1 hour. When roll is nice and firm, cut in 1/4 to 3/16 inch slices. Lay slices on lightly buttered cookie sheets. Bake at 350 degrees for 10 to 12 minutes.

** ** ** ** **

Samuel Adams (1722-1803), signer of the *Declaration of Independence*, was for more than 20 years a Revolutionary leader and patriot in the Colonies. He called for the First Continental Congress. Adams served as a member of this important body until 1881. He wrote: ***"The right to freedom"*** was ***"the gift of the Almighty"*** and that ***"The rights of the colonists as Christians ... may be best understood by reading and studying ... the New Testament."***

Best Recipe of Mrs. Morris for Molasses Cookies

1 cup molasses   1 tsp ginger
1 cup sugar   2 tsp cinnamon
1-⅓ cups warm bacon grease   2 tsp baking soda
1 tsp salt   Flour to suit
                  Sugar as needed

Blend together in a wooden mixing bowl the molasses, sugar and warm bacon grease. Then stir in salt, ginger and cinnamon. Dissolve baking soda in ½ cup boiling water. Add this to mixture in bowl and stir. Lastly begin adding flour and work enough into the mixture to make a soft dough. When ready, dump dough out onto floured board. Roll out to ⅛ to ¼ inch thick sheet. Sprinkle liberally with sugar. Cut with floured cookie cutter or upside down drinking glass. Place cookies on slightly greased cookie sheets. Bake at 350 degrees for 10 to 12 minutes.

** ** ** ** **

Gouverneur Morris (1752-1816) of Philadelphia, Pennsylvania, was a noted delegate to the Constitutional Convention. A Christian, he was the man who wrote the final draft of the *Constitution* and was the originator of the phrase, *"We the People of the United States."* This man was known to be a superb speaker and writer, using his many talents in the discussions that shaped this great document. He spoke 173 times during the debates, more than any other delegate. Gouverneur Morris is the man who served under Robert Morris and managed the finances for the Congress. He is responsible for coming up with the idea of the dollar being used as the basis of American money. Morris was also a member of the Continental Congress as well as a diplomat, statesman and financier. He once wrote: *"Religion is the only solid basis of good morals; therefore education should teach the precepts of religion, and the duties of man toward God."*

Special Raisin Drop Cookies – A Dayton Family Favorite

½ cup butter	3 tsp baking powder
1 cup sugar	2 tsp allspice
2 eggs, well beaten	2 tsp cinnamon
1 cup milk	½ tsp salt
1 tsp vanilla	1 cup nuts, chopped
3 cups flour	2 cups raisins

Using a fork, cream butter and sugar together in a wooden mixing bowl. In a separate bowl, blend eggs, milk and vanilla. In yet a third bowl, sift together the flour, baking powder, allspice, cinnamon and salt. Stir in nuts and raisins. Now add these dry ingredients, and the liquid ingredients, alternately, to the butter-sugar mixture in first bowl. Blend everything thoroughly. Drop from teaspoon onto greased baking sheets. Bake at 375 degrees until cookies are a delicate brown. Makes about 4 dozen 2-inch cookies.

** ** ** ** **

Jonathan Dayton (1760-1824) was a delegate to the Continental Convention in Philadelphia on June 28, 1787. This great Christian patriot was also one of the signers of the *Constitution*. He wrote of how members of the Continental Congress responded to Benjamin Franklin's speech calling for prayer to open Congress each day: " ... ***never did I behold a countenance at once so dignified and delightful as was that of Washington at the close of the address; nor were the members of the convention generally less affected. The words of the venerable Franklin fell upon our ears with a weight and authority ...***" The city of Dayton, Ohio, was named in his honor.

INDEX

ABOUT THE AUTHOR

Robert W. Pelton has been writing for more than 30 years on a great variety of historical and other subjects. He has traveled extensively throughout the world as a researcher and has published hundreds of feature articles and numerous books. Pelton lectures widely, has appeared on many television shows, been a guest on a large number of radio talk shows, and has at one time even hosted his own radio show.

With the unique biographical sketches found in his historical recipe books, he clearly shows how America was unquestionably begun as a Christian nation. He proves beyond doubt that our Founding Fathers — Jefferson, Franklin, Washington, Hancock and the rest — left no question as to their personal beliefs in the *Bible*, the Creator, Salvation and the hand of Providence in the development of out great country and the guidance of its leaders from the very beginning.

Pelton has been in demand as a speaker to diverse groups all over the United States. Tom R. Murray of the Council of Conservative Citizens, after hearing him speak a number of times, offers this: "Mr. Pelton puts together rare combinations of intellectual energies as a writer and speaker that will captivate all levels of an audience. I feel that no one can involve an audience and deliver an important message better than Mr. Robert Pelton."

Pelton may be contacted for convention speaking engagements and for talks before other groups at:

      Freedom & Liberty Foundation
      P.O. Box 12619
      Knoxville, Tn   37912-0619
      Fax: 865-633-8398
         e-mail: cookbooks@juno.com

Historical Thanksgiving Cookery contains the recipes for dishes enjoyed by many Christian signers of the *Declaration of Independence* and heroes of the *Revolutionary War*. Also to be found are the favorite dishes of Christian men and women who wore both the Blue and the Gray during the *War Between the States*. Included is a recipe for Benjamin Franklin's **Molasses Pecan Pie;** the tasty **Tomato Relish** so often enjoyed by the great General Robert E. Lee; Thomas Jefferson's marvelous **English Plum Pudding**; and those wonderful **Sweet Tater Flapjacks** eaten by Stonewall Jackson. All of these men were know to be devout Christians. Each historical recipe is followed by an enlightening biographical sketch. Illustrated.

248 pages $15.95 + $4.50 S&H ISBN 0-7414-1141-5

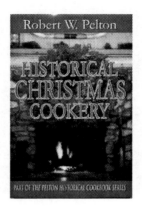

Historical Christmas Cookery is a collection of recipes enjoyed by Christian signers of the *Declaration of Independence* and heroes of the *Revolutionary War*. Included are the favorite dishes of many Christian men and women who wore both the Blue and the Gray during the *War Between the States*. Here will be found the recipe for Benjamin Franklin's **Mashed Turnip and Potato** dish; those **Sour Cream Cookies** so eagerly eaten by the great Jefferson Davis; Patrick Henry's special **French Flannel Cakes**; and the **Boiled Custard** made for Lincoln by his step-mother when he was a boy.. All of these men were known to be devout Christians. Each unique historical recipe is followed by an enlightening biographical sketch. Illustrated.

215 pages $15.95 + $4.50 S&H ISBN 0-7414-1088-5

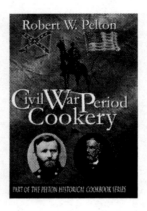

Civil War Period Cookery contains recipes favored by people who lived and loved and prayed during the period of the tragic War Between the States. Included are the favorite dishes of many Christian men and women who fought for both the Union and the Confederacy. Here you will find such recipes as **Brown Sugar Cookies** eaten by General Ulysses S. Grant; a **Pork and Parsnip Stew** dish enjoyed by Medal of Honor winner, Mary Edwards Walker; the **Molasses Pie** made by the mother of Nathan Bedford Forrest; and that special pan of **Giblet-Cornmeal Turkey Stuffing** as it was served to the family of Abner Doubleday. All of these individuals were devout Christians. Each unique historical recipe is followed by an enlightening biographical sketch. Illustrated.

168 pages $13.95 + $4.50 S&H ISBN 0-7414-0971-2

Five or more copies - 40% Discount
Free Shipping on Orders of 20 or More Copies.